Create a happy eater!

The German National Library lists this publication in the German National Bibliography; detailed bibliographic data is available on the Internet at www.dnb.de.

How to Start Solids: Starting Solids for Your Baby with Puree and Finger Foods (The Basic Book for Starting Solid Food and Baby-Led Weaning, Including a 4-Week Guide) by Franka Lederbogen

Studenscheiss GmbH
Oppenhoffallee 143
52066 Aachen, Germany
kontakt@studienscheiss.de
Managing Director: Dr. Tim Reichel, M. Sc.
Registry court: Local Court Aachen
Registration number: HRB 19105
VAT ID No.: DE295455486

1st edition, December 2024

© 2024 veggie + (an imprint of Studienscheiss-Verlag)

ISBN: 978-3-98597-214-2 (Softcover)
ISBN: 978-3-98597-215-9 (Hardcover)
ISBN: 978-3-98597-217-3 (PDF)
ISBN: 978-3-98597-218-0 (EPUB)

Disclaimer: The recipes presented in this book as well as the theoretical explanations on the subject of introducing complementary feeding are the result of the author's practical work. All tips, explanations and recipes described are merely suggestions as to how certain effects can be achieved with certain means. The use and implementation of the described tips are at your own risk. Neither the author nor the publisher accept any responsibility for consequences of any kind whatsoever that have occurred or will occur after the use of one or more of the tips or recipes described.

Copy editing and proofreading: Delia Hansen, Piet Retief
Editor: Hannah Dautzenberg, Aachen
Cover design, layout and typesetting: Tim Reichel, Aachen
Illustration: Jameel Akhtar / vecteezy.com
Photo: Franka Lederbogen, Singapore
Manufacturer: Amazon or a subsidiary
Printed in Germany

Franka Lederbogen

How to Start Solids

Starting Solids for Your Baby with Puree and
Finger Foods (The Basic Book for Starting
Solid Food and Baby-Led Weaning,
Including a 4-Week Guide)

veggie +

Contents

Complementary feeding should be a positive experience for you and your baby. Above all - it should be fun!

Franka on Instagram:

@babyidaeats

Introduction

A happy eater is a good eater

Hi, I'm Franka, mom to two wonderful "baby-led weaning" babies and a nutritionist specializing in baby-friendly complementary foods. Good, healthy and varied food has been my passion for over 20 years. It was clear to me from the very beginning of my life as a mother: The easy and safe introduction of complementary foods for my girls is vital to me. Who wouldn't want to have happy eaters at home?

Since 2019, with my successful blog babyidaisst.com and the Instagram account @babyidaeats, I have helped many parents, whom I support with advice on introducing solid foods. In the same year, I completed further training to become a specialist in baby-friendly complementary feeding with puree and finger foods to build on the content expertise with more scientific facts. My books, instructions, and online courses have already made the start of complementary feeding easier for many parents and helped them to introduce their babies to healthy food in a fun and safe way.

The first year of a baby's life holds many challenges for us as parents. But after having two children and talking to other parents, I came to realize one thing: With common sense, plenty of gut instinct and trust in myself and my competent babies, these challenges can be overcome. Sleepless nights, developmental leaps and all those intense phases in the first few months of life sometimes made me doubt what I was doing and even question my role as a mom. But in the end, the important thing is not to let yourself be unsettled – and this also applies to the introduction of complementary foods.

Nursing follows its own rhythm. Over time, you get the feeling that you understand your baby and have introduced some routine into everyday life. Now, the next new and big topic looms on the horizon: starting solids with thousands of questions and uncertainties.

My daughter Ida didn't want to "work" according to any complementary food plan. This led to frustration and starting solids was anything but fun. The attempt to replace breastfeeding with solids ended in disaster - we both cried. The classic method of introducing complementary foods was simply not for us. There had to be another way. I want to spare you and your baby the stress, frustration, and uncertainty that I went through and give you a method of introducing solid food that will allow you to relax when you start feeding solids to your baby. That's why I wrote this book.

With two girls and my own business, I'm one of those pragmatic mothers. I rarely have time to cook from an elaborate recipe. That's why I've made this book as practical and easy-to-use as possible. This book is designed to show you a simple, healthy and safe way to start complementary feeding. A way that makes the introduction of baby-friendly foods a joy for everyone involved. The aim is for your baby to not only be a happy eater, but also to love healthy food in all its forms.

Important information about the book

I have written this guide to introducing complementary foods because it is time to show a modern way of starting on solids. I want to move away from a rigid feeding schedule that is receiving increasing criticism. Intuitive learning to eat takes into account the individual needs of babies and parents.

I have written this book with great care, based on the knowledge of my training and my decades of experience with healthy nutrition. The recommendations described come from official sources such as the World Health Organization (WHO), UNICEF, the German National Breastfeeding Commission and other experts in German- and English-speaking countries. Nevertheless, this book is not a scientific nutrition guide. It cannot replace a personal visit to a pediatrician or nutritionist for children.

All recipes have been compiled without taking into account individual intolerances and allergies. Therefore, I recommend that you check in advance whether the ingredients in the recipes are suitable for you and your family or whether various foods may need to be substituted.

Let me guide you through every single day with a recipe for nutritional food. I will also give you recommendations for preparing finger food and purees and provide you with information about the individual foods. You will also learn which foods can be combined, which spices go well with them and what variety is appropriate for the first few days.

We start with vegetables and supplement the meals with other healthy foods in order to offer as much variety as possible during this time. I also add meat, dairy products, and allergens. This way, your baby learns right from the start that there is more to food than just carrot and potato puree. Ideally, complementary food could be given about an hour after the last milk feed so that your baby is not too full, but also not too hungry. You should offer baby the usual milk feed after complementary food. This way you continue to provide all the important nutrients. At the same time, digestion is promoted. Basically, it doesn't matter which meal you start with. If possible, start with a meal that the family eats together and that fits in well with your daily routine.

This book of recipes has a modern, sustainable and minimalist design. That's why the publisher and I have dispensed with photos and colorful pictures. However, you still have the opportunity to get a visual idea of all the complementary food recipes, as I have personally made and photographed every complementary food dish. In addition to this book, you will receive a digital photo book from us, in which all the recipes are illustrated.

But that's not all. I have also created each of the food and shopping lists from this book. This way you can save the lists, print them out and take them with you when you go shopping. In addition to that, you will receive my four-week complementary food plan as a print template so that you can hang it up in your kitchen. To make sure that your complementary feeding start is a success, I have also created a clear checklist for you, summarizing the most important points. To get this bonus material, simply click on the link at the end of the book or scan the QR code (Page 183). This will take you to the website of the veggie + publishing house where you can register for the bonus content, free of charge. As an extra you will receive samples of my other cookbooks and can be inspired by the baby-friendly complementary food recipes.

That's it for now. I hope you have lots of fun when you start your baby on solids with the introduction of complementary foods!

The modern way of starting solids

No two starts on solids are the same

Anyone who follows my blog and Instagram account will know that my daughters were not given purees. Instead, I followed an approach that I have had very good experiences with: baby-led weaning (BLW). I will explain exactly what this means in the next chapter. I have also delved into the topic of baby purees through my further training as a specialist in baby-friendly complementary feeding with and without purees.

Even though the introduction of non-pureed complementary foods is on the rise in Europe, the majority of parents still introduce complementary foods according to the classic complementary food schedule. Their babies' first meals in particular consist of puree (often on the advice of pediatricians and midwives). At the time my daughter Ida started her solid food journey, I was almost seen as an exotic figure in my environment with my alternative baby-led weaning approach – although the classic complementary feeding schedule is anything but baby-friendly, as Herbert Renz-Polster describes very vividly in his German blog post "Zoff ums Beifüttern"[1]. Many baby meal plans suggest replacing breast/formula milk feeds with purees far too early, which can lead to early weaning. However, breast/formula milk should remain the most important source of nutrients in the first year of life.

Through conversations with my ever-growing Instagram community, I found out that most parents would prefer to introduce complementary foods with purees and finger food. My approach to introducing solid foods in this book is intended to meet this wish. I want to move away from the step-by-step complementary feeding schedule towards a baby-friendly complementary feeding introduction that is needs-oriented, individual, and based on current findings.

On-demand breast and bottle feeding, is now widespread and established as a recommendation by experts. So why should giving complementary food be any different? With this book, I will show you a way to create an individualized way to introduce solid foods to your baby.

It's about getting to know food, having fun discovering a sense of taste, and learning all the skills needed to eat. Among other things, this lays the foundation for a healthy relationship with food later on in life. I would encourage you to see the introduction of complementary foods as a process in which your baby is given the opportunity to experience food independently and at their own pace. Give your baby the chance to eat independently while taking this journey together.

Myths about starting solids

Before we start with complementary feeding, we must first dispel popular and widespread myths about introducing solids to babies. Many statements and, above all, claims about starting baby on solid food have been around for decades. They are firmly anchored in people's minds, even though they have been refuted for years and are, simply put, wrong.

Myth #1

*All children must start complementary feeding at the same time,
at the age of four months.*

Babies should start complementary foods when they are physiologically ready for them. This maturity is not reached on a calculated day, but over a varied period of time. The baby is most likely ready for solid food between the fifth and seventh month of life.[2] I will go into the right starting point in the next chapters.

Almost all recommendations state that complementary feeding is possible from the fourth or fifth month, but only if the baby is ready for it. The latter part of the statement is often overlooked. Your child and their stage of development determine the start of complementary feeding and not some arbitrary date.

Myth #2

Complementary food means purees

The introduction of complementary foods is done with baby purees, right? If we look at how babies are fed worldwide[3] or travel back 150 years in time, it quickly becomes clear that this cannot be the only way to achieve the goal. After all, the hand blender was only invented in the middle of the 20th century. The fear that a child will choke on food that has not been pureed is therefore a misconception.[4] The human body has the ability to protect itself from choking, even as a baby. More on this in the chapter "Gagging and choking" (page 47).

Myth #3

Introducing solids means spoon feeding

As a continuation of myth no. 2, babies do not need to eat puree or be fed with a spoon. Babies are able to grab baby-friendly modified foods and put them in their mouths from the time they are ready to eat.[5] A spoon held by another person is not absolutely necessary and may pose a risk of choking.[6] You can count on your child's skills. Sure, it takes some practice, and you can't do it without messes. But babies learn to eat with a spoon after just a few months if you let them. They control the amount they want and need to eat. [7]

Myth #4

Solid food replaces breastfeeding or bottle-feeding

The classic solid food schedule suggests this myth without really addressing it. However, it is quite clear that introducing complementary foods and weaning are two different things. Regardless of how you introduce solid food, breast/formula milk remains the most important source of nutrients in the first year of life at least.[8] The amount of puree that a six-month-old baby can eat without initially getting a tummy ache cannot replace the calories and nutrients of a milk meal. As a general rule:

- ✔ Complementary food is not a substitute food!

This is an additional food to the usual milk feed/meal. Babies only start to demand less milk towards the end of the first year of life. More on this in the chapter "Milk feeds and solid foods" (page 37).

Myth #5

Introducing solid food needs a fixed food plan

A plan for the introduction of complementary foods provides a certain amount of security and is not a bad idea in principle. However, a fixed food plan is not necessary. All children are different, eat differently, and like different foods. If your baby is simply different and doesn't follow a plan, this is more frustrating than successful. It is therefore important to find out what works for you.

Myth #6

Babies who eat, sleep better

Probably the most common piece of advice I've received: "Why don't you give her puree for supper, then she'll sleep better". Sleeping and sleeping through the night are developmental steps[9] that may go hand in hand with the introduction of complementary foods. But one has nothing to do with the other. I therefore do not recommend giving your baby a lot of food in the evening in the hope that it will ensure better sleep.

I am sure that you are at least partially aware of these myths. As a rule, such statements and recommendations come from friends and relatives. The people giving the advice often react to a refuting opinion with a personal attack. They have probably followed this advice themselves and clarifying the myths due to new research is tantamount to direct criticism. So, if you get into a conversation like this, keep it in mind. After all, everyone wants the best for their baby and just a few years ago, access to information was not as easy as it is today. What's more, the state of science has also gained new insights in the meantime.

You can stick to your point of view, but also be empathetic towards the person you are talking to and make it clear that you are not criticizing them, but only want the best for your baby.

Starting complementary food

From my own experience and from conversations with other parents, the most difficult part is the start of complementary feeding, i.e. the first meals. Many parents feel insecure here and ask themselves questions such as: Which foods can be offered and in what form? In addition, some of them are particularly worried about details such as the exact amount and the exact time.

What is missing is a clear guide for the first few weeks to give parents the confidence that they know what they are doing. This is what brought about the idea of writing this book with a flexible guide for the first few weeks of introducing complementary foods. Such a guide would have helped me a lot with Ida's complementary feeding.

I wanted to create a guide that is simple and can provide the necessary safety. A guide with baby-friendly foods for the first meals, with information on quantities, food allergies and everything that is not allowed. I had to painstakingly research the answers to my questions. And quite often I was even more confused afterwards than before.

You can rest assured that everything you need to know to start complementary feeding is included in the book and saves you the tedious search that I went through a few years ago. When you use the steps described in this book, you'll build your confidence in offering your baby the right foods after the first four weeks described here. My hope is that you can enjoy eating together.

The basics for your happy eater

Now that we've debunked the starting-on-solid-food myths, you have room for the right mindset to show your child the joy of eating. The following points should always be in the back of your mind when it comes to food for your baby, even well beyond the first few months.

Shared meals

It's as simple as it sounds: One of the most important aspects of eating and babies, is eating together. And yet, it's not uncommon for parents to feed their children before they eat themselves, making a shared meal impossible. We can simply ask ourselves the question: Who likes to eat alone? Nobody - and certainly not your baby. It often turns out that this is precisely the reason for stressful meals and these can be eliminated by eating together.

Shared meals have many advantages. Your baby learns from the family what and how to eat. Babies like to copy the behavior of older children and grown-ups, which includes eating. Over time, your baby will try to pick up the cutlery, fill it with food, push it into their mouth, chew and swallow. Your little one learns how much to take per mouthful and how to drink from a cup - by observing, imitating, and practicing.

It is worth seating your baby at the table before introducing complementary foods. This allows them to observe and learn to eat with a spoon, cup, or plate through play.

Stay relaxed

The more uneasy and stressed you are, the more tense the situation at the dining table will be for your baby. Even if you don't say it out loud, your baby will pick up on the mood with its sensitivity. Ideally, mealtimes should therefore always take place in a relaxed environment. I know - that sounds easier than it is. What can be helpful is setting aside any expectations. Especially in the first year of life, the "how" and "how much" are of secondary importance.

How would you feel if someone sat next to you and watched exactly how much you were eating? Or tries to shove more into you with their spoon without you being able to escape the situation? No one can build a healthy relationship with food under pressure and enjoy the meal. Don't worry so much about getting your child to eat. Instead, make sure they are happy while they join the table - even if it's just playing with the food. A calm environment, without distractions from TV, toys or the like, and a friendly face make a big difference.

Be aware that over the next few months, meals will sometimes go well and sometimes not. Picky eating and complete refusal are part of the development process. On these days, it is of even more important not to put any pressure on yourself or your baby. Give yourselves a break.

Check whether the environment is good and say to yourself: Maybe it will be better tomorrow. Your baby will sometimes eat more, sometimes less and sometimes not at all - but no healthy child will starve itself.

Diversity

Anyone who follows me on Instagram knows that I encourage offering 100 foods in the first year of life. Research shows: The more varied foods are offered in the first few months of complementary feeding, the less picky children are when they get older.[10]

From my own experience, I can say that Ida has never had a phase in which she only ate three different foods. Sure - she loves pasta, preferably only with cheese, and prefers this to many other things. But there are also many other foods that she will eat if I, or even better, if she puts them on her plate herself.

Don't be put off if your baby pulls a face at a new food or pushes it out of their mouth again. Every new taste and texture stimulates the facial muscles. To us, it looks as if the baby is pulling a face because it doesn't taste good. However, this is normal and part of the learning process. It may well be that you have to offer a food ten times before your baby really likes it. So don't give up and keep offering a variety of foods. Be a role model for your baby.

Routine

Similar to putting your baby to bed at night, a mealtime routine can also be useful to prepare your baby for what comes next. Babies like routines. It provides security and supports acceptance of food. This applies to babies and toddlers alike. For example, a routine could consist of being placed in the highchair at the same time every day and having a bib put on. Your baby can then prepare to eat straight away. Such routines also have advantages for you, as they make it easier to keep track of how much and what your child has eaten. If there are snacks here and there and no set or regular mealtimes, it's much harder to keep track.

Every child is different

On some days your baby will ask for seconds twice, on others he or she will probably eat almost nothing at all. Don't let this unsettle you, as this is completely normal. Your own eating behavior certainly also depends on your mood and well-being. Allow your baby to do the same. Don't compare your baby with your friend's or neighbor's baby. Making these comparisons is a trap that parents often fall into. It leads to nothing but pressure and stress, which will only have a negative effect on your baby.

✔ No two babies are the same.

There are big differences between babies' individual eating habits and that's a good thing!

No distractions while eating

Refrain completely from distraction, trickery, bribery, or blackmail at the dining table! This has a negative effect on the natural feeling of hunger and satiety and prevents a healthy relationship with food from developing. In the worst-case scenario, these measures can lead to an eating disorder.[11]

How to introduce solid foods

This chapter is mainly about preparing you for the introduction of complementary foods. You will find out what complementary food is, why babies are given complementary food and when your baby is ready for complementary food. I'll explain how to recognize the signs readiness and give you an introduction to the following three complementary feeding methods:

- ✔ baby-led weaning

- ✔ starting solids with purees

- ✔ the best of both

We look at the topics of milk and solid food as well as the advantages and disadvantages of spoon feeding or independent eating. The most frequently asked questions also revolve around the amount of food, nutrients, drinks, preparation and the biggest concern: choking. I will provide an overview of the foods that are not permitted when introducing complementary foods. I want you to feel confident when preparing the first foods and then offering them to your baby. The following pages contain everything you need to know to get started.

What is complementary food?

Just to be very clear: Complementary food is not there to substitute breast or formula milk - that is a separate topic. Therefore, it is called "complementary food" and not "replacement food". Some rigid complementary food plans are still very widespread, although the gradual replacement of milk meals with puree meals has been considered outdated for many years and has never been scientifically proven to be beneficial.[12] All the more reason for me to write this book.

My first daughter didn't want to follow the "plan" at all. This led to great frustration. It was only after a lot of research that I found out that this is completely normal in the first few months of starting on solids. I learned not to replace milk meals with puree meals and that I should rather follow my gut feeling, my common sense, and the needs of my baby.

You can therefore see complementary feeding as a process of introducing solid foods in a developmentally appropriate way. During this process, you introduce your baby to a variety of foods in small steps. Your task is to regularly provide healthy and varied foods. It is your baby's job to decide what and how much they want to eat. Contrary to many beliefs, your baby knows what it needs.[13] It has the right instincts and protective mechanisms to feed itself. You can give your baby the freedom and support them in learning.

Why complementary food?

In the about first six months of life, a baby only needs breast/formula milk. As it develops and matures physically, it also needs nutrients and energy from other foods, at which point milk alone is no longer sufficient.[14]

Nevertheless, breast/formula milk remains a main component of the daily diet. At twelve months, it can still make up 50% or even more of the daily requirement.[15] However, as babies first have to learn to eat and this is a process that takes several months, it is advisable to start introducing complementary foods when they are ready. Eating is a skill that has to be learned, just like turning over, crawling, talking and walking. And here too, practice makes perfect. Introducing solid foods helps to teach skills such as chewing, swallowing, and drinking.

The intestines also need exercise to digest solid food. The intestinal flora continues to develop, and digestive enzymes need to be formed. This can be clearly seen in the results in the diaper after the first complementary meals. You will probably notice that the first chunks of food end up in the diaper just as they were swallowed. But after a few weeks, digestion will improve and it will be difficult to tell what your baby has eaten. The color will change and can vary depending on the food eaten. For example, the stool will turn almost black after blueberries or dark green after spinach.

Proper nutrition in infancy has a positive effect on health. It is an important foundation for physical growth and brain development. The variety of different foods, tastes and textures that a baby is allowed to try in the first year of life has an influence on their later preference for certain foods.[16]

When should I start complementary foods?

The "when" is one of the biggest questions parents ask themselves when introducing solid foods. In this current age, complementary foods are introduced later than they were a few years ago. This is because introducing foods too early can have negative consequences later on.[17] The regular introduction of solids is only safe once a certain stage of development has been reached. This means that it is difficult to introduce complementary foods before the baby is ready to eat, as the baby's oral motor skills are not sufficiently developed to be able to eat from a spoon, let alone independently. In addition, the digestive tract is still immature at this early stage and complementary foods can overload the kidneys and intestines. This means that the nutrients from solid foods cannot be optimally utilized, and, in the worst case, allergies may even develop.[18]

Most babies are physiologically ready for solids around the sixth month.[19] However, the answer to the question of "when" cannot be answered with an exact number, but with the achievement of developmental milestones. So instead of focusing on monthly or weekly figures, you can pay attention to your baby's development, as this is different for every child. The World Health Organization and UNICEF have defined three signs of maturity that you can use as a guide.[20] If your baby meets these signs of maturity, it is ready for its first complementary food. These signs of readiness apply to baby purees as well as baby-led weaning or a combination of these methods.

Why do some products say "from the fourth month"?

Even though the WHO has adopted a non-binding "International Code of Marketing of Breast-milk Substitutes", companies in many countries do not adhere to it. From the company's point of view, more sales can be achieved through this recommendation and the code is not legally binding yet.[21]

The three signs of readiness

In this section, I will illustrate what the three maturity signs of being ready for solids are and how you can recognize your baby's readiness.[22]

Sign #1: sitting

- ✔ Can your baby hold his head stable and sit alone in the high-chair or with light support on your lap without slumping? Then you have already met the first milestone.

Signs #2: eye-hand-mouth coordination

- ✔ Does baby's eye-hand-mouth coordination work? Does your baby focus on something with their eyes, reach for it and then put it in their mouth? In this case, the second indicator for readiness is fulfilled too.

Sign #3: tongue thrust reflex

- ✔ Is your baby's tongue thrust reflex weakening? You can test this by placing a finger on the lower lip and seeing if your baby tries to push it away with the tongue. If this reflex decreases, then your baby has fulfilled the third milestone of being ready for solid foods.

When your baby has fulfilled all three signs and also shows an interest in food, you can start introducing complementary foods.

In the first few months of complementary feeding, solid food is only a supplement to breast/formula milk. A widespread misconception is that breast milk no longer contains enough iron from the sixth month onwards. This assertion is not true, across the board. Children born under normal circumstances are still supplied with sufficient iron from breast/formula milk after the sixth month.[23]

There are many signs of readiness in circulation, but only these three developmental signs really indicate the physical ability to safely eat and digest solid food. Until your baby is not physiologically ready to digest solid food, you should not offer solid food. In any case, wait for these maturity characteristics before you offer food other than breast/formula milk for the first time. This way you can be sure that your child and their body are truly ready for complementary foods.

Please remember: Despite these physical signs of maturity, some babies may not show any real interest in food until they are eight months old and prefer to go back to their usual milk. Don't push your baby to do anything that it doesn't allow on its own.

Starting solids with purees

Baby's readiness as explained above is the signal for starting complementary food. Baby purees are a good option to start with. This works well for some, but not at all for others.

It is important to realize that complementary food is not a substitute for baby's usual milk. At least not in the first months in. And here is why: In the beginning a puree meal never has as many nutrients and calories as a milk feed. 100 ml of breast milk has around 70 kcal. By contrast, 100 g of vegetable puree has just half that. In addition, a baby of six months can easily drink 100 ml of breast /formula milk, but it is very unlikely that they will be able to eat 100 g of puree straight away. [24]

There is nothing wrong with introducing complementary foods with puree or common baby puree recipes. The different approach is not following a rigid plan, but rather paying attention to your baby's needs and offer significantly more variety. Learning to eat is a complex process of physical skills which takes months to achieve. Breast/formula milk remains an important source of nutrients in the first year of life, unless your baby wants to drink less milk of their own accord. If you opt for puree, that's great and you can reap all the benefits. Listen to yourself and your baby's needs.

If you want to offer puree, you don't necessarily have to feed your baby. You can fill the spoon for your baby and then let them feed themselves. In the chapter "Responsive feeding and eating independently" (page 40) you can find out more about this.

The great thing is that you don't have to choose between puree and another method. In the next chapter, I'll explain the concepts of baby-led weaning. And a combination of all methods is always possible too.

Baby-led weaning

Baby-led weaning (BLW) is not as new as it is often described. This method of introducing complementary foods is probably as old as mankind itself. It existed long before blenders and baby purees.

It is an approach to introducing solid foods which skips the start with purees and goes straight to proper foods. Furthermore, the baby self-feeds and caregivers do not spoon-feed. The baby therefore determines the time of weaning and the start of complementary feeding. Traditional feeding with only baby purees is avoided. It does not exclude the eating of puree-like foods such as mashed potatoes or puree.

The idea behind this is that babies eat independently from the time they are ready for solids. Parents only take on the task of preparing food in a baby-friendly way and offering as much variety as possible. Ideally, babies eat directly at the family table. This method of introducing complementary foods has been scientifically investigated, with impressive results.[25]

Clara M. Davis began an experiment in 1928 and allowed babies ready to eat solid food to choose their own food from 33 healthy foods. Each child chose different foods for themselves and changed their choice if they were ill, for example. They also tried almost everything. None of the children were found to be malnourished.[26] It is therefore not surprising that children eat as differently as they are unique. After all, we adults do the same. One could therefore assume that babies know what they need.

The criticism of BLW that there is a risk of nutrient deficiency has been refuted and is unjustified. As long as milk feeds are not reduced in contrast to the baby's needs, optimal nutrient supply is guaranteed.

Letting a baby eat independently has many advantages:

- ✔ The baby can learn to eat through play.

- ✔ The baby practices important motor skills.

- ✔ It promotes independence and gives the baby control.

- ✔ It encourages self-control because your baby can stop when it is full. This prevents overfeeding.

- ✔ It reduces later problems with obesity.[27]

- ✔ It simplifies meal preparation, because babies usually like to eat what the grown-ups eat.

- ✔ It can avoid the development of picky eating behavior due to the variety of different foods and textures.

- ✔ It strengthens the family feeling through shared meals, and at the same time, learning through imitating.

One disadvantage of BLW from my own experience is the mess that is present at every meal for the first few months. But, as they get older, it becomes less and less. Another disadvantage is the fact that at the beginning you can only estimate what has actually been eaten. However, in the end, the proof can at least be found in the diaper.

For most parents I have spoken to, the concept of BLW is somewhat unfamiliar. They often don't have the confidence to give their baby so much responsibility. Also, not everyone trusts their baby's ability to eat finger food from the point of readiness for solids. Many therefore resort to a slightly modified version or a complementary food mix of finger food and puree so as not to give up control completely.

And there is basically nothing to be said against it. The first few weeks can be particularly nerve-wracking, but over time most parents become braver and trust their babies more. It is important to always pay attention to your baby's signs, meet their needs and respect their boundaries.

As already explained, you don't have to decide on one complementary feeding method straight away, as a combination is also an option. The important thing is that you find out what works for you in everyday family life. That's why you'll find a complementary food recipe for each day in the chapter "The first 4 weeks" (page 65), which includes both the preparation for finger food and for puree. This way you always have the option to choose - or what I would recommend: Always offer both options. This will not only teach you which complementary food you can prepare and how, but also what works best for you and your baby.

Milk feeds and solid foods

Breast/formula milk should be the sole source of nutrition until the baby is ready for complementary food. When the baby shows all signs of readiness, solid foods can be slowly introduced in addition to the usual infant milk meals. Breastfeeding or bottle feeding on demand ensure optimal nutrition and can be continued beyond the second year of life if needed.[28]

In addition to the complementary food myths, there is also the myth that the nutrients in breast milk are no longer sufficient for babies from the sixth month onwards and therefore solid food must be given. This myth arose from a study that investigated which amount of meat in a baby-food jar provides a better iron supply. Although the result was that different, amounts of meat in the puree had no influence on the iron supply, a partial result was published in favor of the meat industry, which showed that breast milk contains less iron than infant formula. This led to the misinterpretation that breastfed babies are at risk of an iron deficiency and that they should start with meat puree at an early age. However, the fact is that the iron in breast milk can be metabolized particularly well by the body and therefore the amount consumed via breast milk is sufficient. There is therefore generally no risk of iron deficiency for breastfed children.[29]

It is true that nutrient reserves such as zinc and iron from the womb are used up by the baby after a few months. However, a baby gets the nutrients it needs from infant milk. It is also interesting to note that the average composition of breast milk in terms of nutrient content in the sixth month of life does not differ from breast milk in the 24th month of life.[30] Therefore:

- ✔ Breast/formula milk remains an important source of nutrients in the first year of life and beyond![31]

When breastfeeding, it is difficult to tell how much milk your baby is really drinking. That's why I recommend paying attention to your baby's signs and breastfeeding on demand. Because your baby knows what it needs.

In the first few months of baby-friendly solids, the milk requirement will not change noticeably. When your baby starts to crawl and becomes more mobile, it may well be that the milk requirement remains the same despite two to three additional meals a day being offered. The increased movement leads to an increased energy requirement. As soon as this has settled down, you will notice that the amount of milk your baby requires slowly decreases. This can happen at ten months, but also around the first birthday. Many children like their usual milk beyond the first year of life and that's fine.

To ensure your baby's nutrient supply during the introduction of complementary foods, it can be useful to offer breast/formula milk to your baby 30 to 60 minutes before and 30 to 60 minutes after the complementary meal. This will ensure that your baby is not too hungry to concentrate on the complementary food and that they can drink their fill of usual milk after the complementary food. This is what a daily schedule with the first complementary meal can look like:

6:30 a.m.	breast/formula milk
9:00 a.m.	breast/formula milk
11:30 a.m.	breast/formula milk
12:30 p.m.	**complementary food + breast/formula milk**
3:00 p.m.	breast/formula milk
5:30 p.m.	breast/formula milk
8:00 p.m.	breast/formula milk

You can use this example to introduce the first complementary meal. The times depend on your breastfeeding/bottle feeding rhythm. The timing should also fit into your daily routine and does not necessarily have to be at lunchtime. It is important that milk is not replaced by complementary food unless your baby refuses its usual milk of its own accord.

During the introduction of complementary foods, there may always be phases in which more milk is drunk and less complementary food is eaten. The causes are usually new teeth, growth spurts, infections or similar. Many parents tell me that the amount of food eaten stagnates or even decreases, especially in the eighth and ninth month. Don't let this unsettle you and stick to your routine.

Responsive feeding and eating independently

The usual baby puree method goes hand in hand with spoon feeding. The classic BLW method, on the other hand, recommends having absolutely no influence on what ends up in your baby's mouth. Letting your child eat independently is beneficial to their development. However, many parents do not feel comfortable leaving food intake entirely up to the child. A mixture of both approaches may be an acceptable method in this case.

Studies have shown that independent eating helps babies and children to develop healthy eating behavior, especially in terms of quantity. Spoon-feeding is not necessary. Independent eating helps to learn all the skills needed for eating and strengthens independence. It also encourages a positive relationship with food and different foods, which helps to pass through later normal phases of food refusal more easily. Familiarization with family meals takes place much earlier, as parents of independent eaters are quicker to offer some of their own food.[32] The big advantage of independent eating is that the parents also get to eat, as the baby is busy.

Whether independent eating or spoon-feeding works for you depends mainly on your baby. Some babies prefer to be fed. They open their mouths expectantly to get the next morsel. Others close their mouths tightly and turn away. They prefer to eat on their own. Pay attention to your baby's signals, because they will show you what they like best. I would always recommend letting your baby eat on their own because of the advantages mentioned above, but if you notice that your baby really wants to be fed, then you can do this too. After all, it is a form of attention and attention is a need that you should always fulfill for your baby.

However, still offer an option for independent eating in the form of finger food or a filled spoon. If you opt for puree but would like your baby to eat independently, use two or three spoons, fill them with puree and place them in front of your baby one after the other so that they can grab the spoon independently and bring it to their mouth.

In fact, I always recommend independent eating. It is very likely that your baby will only play with the food at the beginning; crush it with their hands, smear it on the table, put it in their mouth and spit it out again or throw it on the floor. This is completely normal and is part of the learning process. Stay relaxed and give your baby the space to explore. This usually goes away after a few meals. The only exception to this is when we are visiting or in a restaurant and mealtime is otherwise not possible without mess and chaos.

Is my child eating enough?

For some parents, the fear that their child is not eating enough is dominant. Often the reason is a previous history related to their baby's weight. There can be many reasons for this. Here are some examples in which you may recognize yourself and your baby:

- ✔ Your baby was particularly light after birth.

- ✔ There were problems with breast or bottle feeding in the first few months.

- ✔ You have received inappropriate comments from friends or relatives about your baby's weight because your baby was very slim.

As parents, we always want the best for our little ones and it is not uncommon for us to be so strongly influenced by external factors that we question our common sense. If you also feel this uncertainty, remember your gut feeling and common sense and pay attention to your baby's needs.[33] Get the misconception that "babies and children don't know what's good for them" out of your head.

Babies have a natural instinct regarding satiation. As a rule, they do not overfeed themselves with breast/formula milk but stop when they are full. This was also shown by Dr. Clara Davis' experiment.[34]

The simple answer to the frequently asked question "How much does my baby need to eat to be full and get enough nutrients?" is therefore:

- ✔ Your baby can eat as much or as little as it likes.

Don't stick to the number of grams that the puree manufacturer writes on the jar or the specification in the complementary feeding schedule. Don't look to other babies as examples.

Your baby can and should eat exactly as much as it likes, because: every baby is different. There are no quantities that guarantee that your baby will be sufficiently supplied with nutrients. Eating is individual and intuitive, even for babies.

Breastfeeding and bottle-feeding on demand have become widely established. This raises the question: Why should the intake of complementary foods be strictly scheduled? If babies can decide for themselves when they drink how much milk, why not when and how much solid food they eat?

Your baby will concentrate on the meal and take what they need - as long as they are in an undisturbed and comfortable environment. This can also be minimal amounts that you think will never be enough. However, as breast/formula milk remains an important source of nutrition in the first year, you don't need to worry about sufficient nutrients for the time being.

If your baby is still not interested in food at nine months and won't even try a small amount, you can have the iron level checked by your pediatrician. Loss of appetite is a symptom of iron deficiency, which you can rule out or counteract at an early stage.[35] A shortened frenum of the tongue (also known as a tongue-tie) could be another reason for this.

Signs of hunger and satiety

Babies know when they are full. Even if they have only eaten three spoons of puree or half a vegetable stick, they may have finished their meal. Pay attention to the signals your baby gives you. It sounds simple - and it is. To make it easy for you to find out what these signs might be, I'll give you a few examples here:

Possible signs that your baby wants to eat more:

- ✔ Your baby opens its mouth.

- ✔ Your baby points to the food.

- ✔ Your baby reaches for the food.

- ✔ Your baby leans towards the food or spoon.

- ✔ Your baby tries to reach for your food.

- ✔ Your baby cries when the plate is empty or you stop feeding.

Possible signs that your baby is full:

- ✔ Your baby presses its lips together.

- ✔ Your baby turns its head away.

- ✔ Your baby leans/stretches on the highchair.

- ✔ Your baby pushes the plate or bowl away.

- ✔ Your baby throws food down or clears food off the plate.

- ✔ Your baby is crying and signaling resistance.

Nutrients and digestion

Nutrients are important, no question about it. However, the whole topic of nutrient supply is one that shouldn't make you feel too insecure. After all, you can ensure a healthy nutrient intake with just a few simple rules. So, you don't need to be a nutrition expert to provide your baby with the right nutrients. Let me start by briefly explaining the most important nutrients. These are:

- carbohydrates
- fats
- proteins

Every meal should contain these three ingredients for your baby. Other important nutrients for your child's development include

- vitamin C
- iron
- calcium
- omega-3 fatty acids
- zinc[36]

Don't worry! Your baby's feeding plan doesn't have to include all these nutrients in every meal. I have a simpler system for you to follow to ensure a nutritious diet.

This will ensure that your diet is rich in nutrients:

- ✔ Make sure that the meal contains two to three different colors so that there is a colorful selection on the baby's plate. Instead of only offering white pasta, you should supplement it with red sauce and green herbs.

- ✔ Offer diverse and varied meals.

- ✔ Use less processed food. Avoid ready-made baked goods, for example, and make them yourself instead.

- ✔ Use lots of fresh vegetables and fruit.

- ✔ Avoid ready meals and fast food.

- ✔ Continue to offer breast/formula milk as it covers all the necessary nutrients.

In the chapter "A balanced baby plate" (page 145), I explain how you can fill a nutrient-rich baby plate. At the end of this book, you will also find a list of suitable foods for complementary foods (page 157).

Gagging and choking

When I talk to parents about introducing complementary foods without purees, the first reaction is often: "I'd be afraid that my baby would choke." If you share this concern, I would like to allay your fears in this chapter. First of all: Feeding puree does not protect your child from choking. Babies are no less likely to choke on puree than on finger food.[37] Puree that has been swallowed, i.e. inhaled, is much harder to cough up than baby-friendly solid food such as finger food.[38] If the spoon is not guided by the baby, the baby has no control over how far the spoon reaches into the mouth and how much food ends up in the mouth.

Let's start by clarifying the difference between choking and gagging. These two terms are not the same, even though they are often used interchangeably. Here is the distinction:

1. The gag reflex is the natural protection mechanism against choking.

2. A baby who gags has not necessarily choked.

3. Gagging does not lead to choking because the windpipe is closed during this process.

4. Gagging is part of learning how to eat.

There are a few signs by which you can recognize whether your baby is gagging or choking.

How to recognize gagging:[39]

- ✔ Your baby sticks his tongue out and tries to push the food out.

- ✔ Your baby's face turns red.

- ✔ You hear gagging noises and coughing.

- ✔ Your baby is vomiting.

How to recognize choking:[40]

- ✔ Your baby's face turns blue.

- ✔ Your baby becomes still and falls silent.

- ✔ Coughing does not help or is not possible.

The gag reflex keeps the airways clear and is an important mechanism that occurs automatically in your baby. You should not intervene, as this could only make things worse. I know how hard it is to stay calm, but: let your baby do it, it will master the situation.

If your baby is choking, it's a different story: This is when you need to take the steps you may have learned on a first aid course for children. However, the likelihood of serious choking is low. The most common cause of choking in children is small non-food object and food that is not prepared in a baby-friendly way.

The following facts about choking and complementary foods will hopefully allay some of your fears:

- ✔ Introducing complementary foods with finger food from the time your baby is ready to be fed is just as safe as with baby puree. There is no increased risk of choking.[41]

- ✔ The gag reflex protects your baby from choking when they are ready to eat solid food. This becomes weaker over time, which is why it makes sense and is safer to offer foods of all textures from the time your baby is ready to eat rather than only when he is a toddler.[42]

- ✔ The windpipe of a baby has approximately the diameter of a straw. Large pieces of food will not get stuck there.[43]

- ✔ With your baby, either only the esophagus or the windpipe is open, never both at the same time. The likelihood of food getting into the windpipe is therefore low. In addition, in a rare case, puree can enter the windpipe just as quickly as solid food.

 Studies have shown that food is safest for both babies and adults when they eat it on their own. How would we feel if a spoon was shoved into our mouth out of nowhere? We would probably be startled. For babies, this experience is even more intense.[44]

It is normal for your baby to gag on complementary food and is part of learning to eat. Gagging is the natural protective mechanism that prevents babies from choking. The more you let your baby practice eating, the quicker it will learn to gag less. There are always babies who vomit due to gagging. As unpleasant as it is to observe this, it is normal and nothing to worry about.

For a safe start to the complementary feeding period, I have compiled a list of rules in the following chapter to minimize the risk of serious choking or suffocation.

Rules for the safe introduction of complementary foods

To make you feel even safer, there are a few simple rules for the safe start on solid food that will help minimize the risk of serious choking. Use this checklist to ensure a safe introduction of complementary foods:

- ✔ Wait with the introduction of solid foods until all three signs of readiness have been met (page 31).

- ✔ Only let your baby eat sitting upright, never lying down or reclining. No feeding in a baby bouncer or baby car seat, for example.

- ✔ Use a highchair with a footrest, as a firm support for the feet makes it easier to cough or offer solids while your baby is sitting on your lap.

- ✔ Prepare the food that it can be easily squished between your thumb and index finger. This ensures that the consistency is so soft that your baby's palate, tongue, and chewing ridges can easily crush the food, even without teeth.

- ✔ Do not offer food that is unsuitable for babies (page 51).

- ✔ Never leave your baby unattended while eating.

- ✔ For a more confidence, you can take a children's first aid course.

- ✔ It will help your baby to learn to eat if you demonstrate biting, chewing, and swallowing.

- ✔ Stay calm! It can be scary when your baby starts to gag. This is normal when learning to eat and you shouldn't react frighteningly to it, as this could also frighten your baby.

Suitable and unsuitable foods for babies

The question of which foods should and should not be offered as complementary foods is very important when it comes to starting solids. The list of unsuitable foods is relatively short. For some foods, there are instructions for preparation that you should follow. Below you will find a summary of the most important information.

Which complementary foods are suitable?

Almost all foods are permitted in a baby-friendly form. Babies are able to eat almost all family meals from the complementary food stage, as long as they are prepared in a baby-friendly way.

Suitable complementary foods are those that can be easily crushed between the index finger and thumb. Your baby will then be able to crush this food between the palate and tongue and then swallow it.

There are a few foods that your baby should not eat at all. Others, on the other hand, require preparation to make them safe and suitable for babies. I have created an overview for you:

What your baby shouldn't eat:

- honey and maple syrup (risk of bacteria that release the toxin botulinum toxin in the intestine)

- raw eggs (such as in home-made mayonnaise)

- raw meat and raw fish (risk of salmonella or bacterial infection)

- raw milk products (risk of bacterial infection)

- ✔ coffee, green and black tea, or other beverages containing caffeine/thein

- ✔ whole nuts and seeds

- ✔ popcorn and candy (high risk of choking)

- ✔ salt (with a maximum 1 g of salt per day, avoid additional salt when preparing dishes and make sure that the salt content of purchased foods is low)

- ✔ industrial sugar, artificial sweeteners, and flavorings

- ✔ fast food and convenience products

- ✔ alcohol

What your baby can eat:

- ✔ plump, elastic foods such as berries, grapes, beans, olives and peas mashed, finely chopped, or pureed

- ✔ nuts as butter or nut flour

- ✔ leaf lettuce, leaf herbs, and spinach, finely chopped or pureed (could otherwise stick to the palate)

- ✔ cabbage, cooked, chopped, or pureed

- ✔ hard vegetables and fruit (such as apple, pear, cucumber or carrot) cooked (otherwise there is a risk of choking)

- ✔ food with a coarse cell structure such as lettuce and most cabbage cooked and chopped or pureed, otherwise only when molars are present

With a few exceptions, your baby can also eat all spices from the time they are ready for complementary food. It even has advantages for later eating behavior if your baby can get used to spices at an early age. Both dried and fresh herbs are ideal for getting your baby used to spicy food at an early age. Just try out what your baby likes.

Suitable spices for babies, in moderation:

- ✔ fresh and dried green herbs
- ✔ mild pepper
- ✔ turmeric
- ✔ ginger
- ✔ cumin
- ✔ coriander
- ✔ sweet bell pepper
- ✔ ceylon cinnamon
- ✔ vanilla
- ✔ cardamom
- ✔ mild curry powder
- ✔ aniseed
- ✔ allspice
- ✔ carnations

Nutmeg, saffron, and cassia cinnamon can be dangerous for babies, children and adults in large quantities.

Spices not recommended for babies:

- ✔ salt
- ✔ sugar substitutes
- ✔ flavoring
- ✔ chilli
- ✔ other hot spices

Food allergies

The currently revised guideline for allergy prevention (in Germany) also recommends starting complementary foods between the fifth and seventh month of life and continuing breastfeeding beyond the introduction of complementary foods.[45] It is assumed that the best prevention of food allergies is to introduce allergens under the protection of breast milk. Breastfeeding can therefore help to prevent allergies during the introduction of solid foods.[46]

It is also recommended to offer a variety of complementary foods right from the start. This includes fish, dairy products, and properly cooked eggs. It is therefore not necessary to introduce one food several days in a row or to introduce allergens late.

Babies who are given infant formula are not necessarily more likely to have allergies. The most important prerequisite is a healthy intestinal flora. This is because food allergies develop in the gut, even if the allergy manifests itself on the skin.[47] This wrongly identifies a certain food as dangerous and reacts defensively.

Science is still unable to explain in detail exactly how food allergies develop. However, it is clear that a mature gut and healthy intestinal flora with as many different bacteria as possible result in fewer allergies. There is also a connection between excessive cleanliness and an increased risk of allergies.[48]

What allergens are there?

The following list[49] contains foods that can cause allergies and intolerances:

- ✔ dairy and dairy products (lactose)

- ✔ eggs

- ✔ fish and shellfish

- ✔ peanuts

- ✔ nuts such as almonds, hazelnuts, walnuts and others

- ✔ grains containing gluten, such as wheat, rye, barley, oats, spelt and others

- ✔ soybeans and soy products

- ✔ celery

- ✔ mustard

- ✔ sesame seeds

- ✔ lupine seeds

- ✔ molluscs

Tips how to introduce common food allergens

1. Start with very small amounts such as a tip of a teaspoon of the allergen mixed in baby's food. The smaller the quantity the less severe an allergic reaction may be. If there is no reaction continue to offer it regularly and increase the amount of the allergen.

2. When introducing an allergen the first time, do it early in the day and not before naptime. This way you can be aware of any symptoms should there be a reaction.

3. Test one allergen at the time and only with already introduced food which have shown no reaction. This way, you can be sure which food caused a reaction.

4. Once you started to introduce a food allergen offer it in regular rotations, as this was found to be effective allergy prevention.

How can you recognize a food allergy or intolerance?

An allergy or intolerance usually manifests itself in babies through a skin rash, swelling of the face, coughing or reactions of the digestive tract, such as vomiting or diarrhea,[50] which would appear within about a couple of hours after contact.

If you have a well-founded concern about an allergy, perhaps due to family background, then you can test the suspected foods separately from other complementary foods. It may be worth talking to an allergist or a pediatrician if you are worried about an allergy, but especially if there has been an allergic reaction.

Beverages other than milk

As soon as you start complementary feeding, you can also offer small amounts of water, for example from a shot glass. Use water that is considered safe for drinking in your area.

In the beginning, the purpose of drinking water is only to teach your baby to drink from a cup or small glass. It is not intended to provide your baby with sufficient fluids. Optimal hydration is still provided by breast/formula milk. In the first year of life, the amount of water drunk should not exceed 200 ml per day, otherwise there is a risk of water intoxication or overhydration.[51]

Unless otherwise prescribed by your doctor or nutritionist, you can offer the following amounts of water with your meals:

- ✔ from the start of complementary feeding until about nine months, no more than 100 ml daily

- ✔ at nine to twelve months no more than 200 ml per day

- ✔ from the first birthday at least 200 ml daily up to 1 L, depending on how much breast/formula milk is consumed[52]

Please bear in mind that these are average figures and are intended as a guide only. Ultimately, the amount of water your baby drinks depends on its individual needs. However, in the first year of life, I always recommend offering breast/formula milk over normal water for hydration.

Juice, soft drinks, teas, and milk that is not breast milk or infant formula should generally not be on a baby's or toddler's daily beverage plan. For us adults, it may be boring to drink only still water. However, if your child doesn't know any differently, it won't be like that. Herbal teas can have a medicinal effect that could be lost if the tea is drunk every day. Fruit teas contain acid, which is harmful to milk teeth as it attacks the tooth enamel. This also applies to sugary drinks such as juice, soft drinks, and milk alternatives. Constantly letting teeth come into contact with these beverages will sooner or later lead to tooth decay.

Sugary drinks are not only bad for your teeth, but also for your general health and can contribute to overweight and obesity. Avoid zero drinks, they contain artificial sweetener which are not suitable for babies. Water is therefore completely sufficient for practicing drinking.[53]

Small open cups and glasses for at home and straw cups for on the go are best suited as drinking containers.

Complementary food equipment

Basic kitchen equipment such as a fork, spoon, knife, bowl, chopping board and saucepan are all you need to start complementary feeding. Of course, there are a few things that are a good addition and make it easier to prepare daily meals and deal with any mess. That's why I'd like to introduce you to my baby food kit below, which I used to start with complementary foods to my babies without any problems.

Highchair with tray and footrest

The right position is essential when learning to eat. A highchair with footrests, where your baby can easily reach the tray and footrest is a real help when introducing solid foods. Sitting in a stable position is important to be able to cough properly when gagging. One of my favorites is the Stokke TRIPP TRAPP® highchair. The Hauck "Alpha" highchair is suitable for those on a budget and also fulfills its purpose. If you place more value on design at the dining table, the "Nomi" highchair could be suitable for you. In my opinion, the IKEA ANTILOP highchair without footrests is not a particularly safe choice for babies who are only just ready to eat.

Bib with sleeves and belly pocket

If you don't want to buy new clothes by the dozen, a good bib is an absolute must. Because spills and splatters are common in the beginning; unfortunately many foods don't wash well out of certain fabrics. Banana and avocado, for example, have already ruined some of Ida's bodysuits. The bibs with sleeves and pocket over the belly were therefore indispensable for me. Additional to the benefit of clean clothes, less food is wasted because the little ones can easily reach for any food that has fallen into the pocket.

Plate and bowl with good grip

Babies don't just play with food, they also like to examine the dishes and sometimes drop them. Some foods can be placed directly on the tabletop, but muesli, for example, is better in a bowl or a deep plate with sufficient grip on the table. The plates and bowls from ezpz and Bamboo Bamboo have proved their worth in our home.

Drinking cup

To get your baby used to drinking properly, a small cup or glass will do. We use the drinking cup from ezpz at home. After a little practice, Ida learned to drink from it relatively quickly without spilling too much. The advantage of this cup is that it is weighted at the bottom so that it doesn't fall over so easily if the baby bumps it. An open cup should always be the first choice for water. A leak-proof bottle with a straw is best for on the go.

Cutlery

In the beginning, your baby will naturally eat their solids with their fingers. Nevertheless, you don't have to do completely without cutlery at the table - after all, practice makes perfect. A small spoon ideal for baby hands that your baby can hold well is best for this. Try out different types of cutleries and give a metal teaspoon a try.

Storage container

Especially at the beginning, your baby will only eat a little and a lot will end up on the floor. That's why it makes sense to only ever offer a small selection of food and keep the rest in the fridge or freezer in suitable containers. I recommend glass containers because they are hygienic and don't absorb unpleasant odors.

Floor protection mat

Particularly in the first few months of introducing complementary feeding, it can get quite messy as the little ones love to play with their food - and they are allowed to do so. To protect the floor and make it easier to clean up afterwards, a floor protection mat under the highchair has proved very useful for us. It's best to look for a mat that is roughly the size of your baby's throwing circle.

Steamer

Foods that are soft are ideal for starting complementary foods without baby purees. For example, potatoes, carrots, zucchinis, meats, or even fish can be prepared particularly gently by steaming without losing many vitamins. An adjustable steamer insert for pots makes it particularly easy to prepare small quantities of food. I use this piece of equipment almost every day.

Washable wipes

To deal with the mess mentioned above, you should always have a washcloth for the table and one for the floor at hand. Washable cloths are better for the environment than wet wipes.

Preparation and storage

Baby food, whether puree or finger food, should be prepared in a baby-friendly way. This means in a consistency that babies can crush and swallow even without teeth. The two-finger squeeze rule states that the food must be able to be squished between the thumb and index finger. With this rule, you are always on the safe side.

To avoid contamination and protect your baby from illness, proper hygiene is important when preparing food. Make sure kitchen surfaces and utensils are clean. Wash your hands before preparing food and your baby's hands before meals. Also make sure that you wash ingredients such as fruit, vegetables, fruit, meat and fish thoroughly before you process them. Keep raw foods such as meat, fish, and eggs separate from other foods before preparing them. This prevents the transfer of bacteria that may be present in raw food.

How to prepare

The following preparation methods are suitable for the baby-friendly preparation of food:

- steaming (in a pot with steamer insert or in a steamer)
- boiling
- baking
- roasting
- deep frying

To retain as many nutrients as possible when cooking, I prefer steaming, boiling and baking. However, there is also nothing to be said against the use of a microwave oven to reheat dishes or ingredients. You can also offer your baby fried or deep-fried food to provide enough variety in the preparation.

These methods of preparation are not as gentle as steaming, boiling, and baking, but as long as you keep everything in balance, you can also prepare baby-friendly foods in this way.

Storage

Especially in the beginning of complementary feeding, babies only eat small amounts and it is rarely worth preparing just one or two baby portions. That's why I recommend pre-cooking larger quantities and storing them in the fridge or freezer. The pre-cooked dishes can be kept fresh in a sealed container and stored in the fridge for about three days. The shelf life always depends on the ingredients. You can keep the following in mind:

- Pureed food can be kept fresh in a sealed container for about three days in the fridge or frozen for up to six months.

- Cooked dishes will keep for about three days in the fridge and for about six months in the freezer. Ideally, you should freeze them in portions to make defrosting easier.

- Some types of fruit can also be stored in the fridge or freezer. However, for the best taste, I recommend always cutting them up fresh.

The first 4 weeks

Starting on solids step by step

Are you and your baby ready for complementary food? Great, then let's make a happy eater out of your baby! This chapter will guide you step by step through the first four weeks of introducing solid foods with and without purees. However, don't feel obliged to follow everything 100% according to plan. If you don't manage to offer solids, a day's break in between is absolutely no problem. For example, you could also offer the following recipes two days in a row and turn the four-week plan into an eight-week plan.

This is a guide for every single day. I'll give you recommendations for preparation and provide you with information about the individual foods. In the next sections I'll show you which foods can be combined, which spices go well with them and what variety is appropriate in the first few days.

You do not necessarily need to add oil to the food. Your baby gets the fats needed to utilize the nutrients from the breast/formula milk. However, for your baby to get used to some oil and also become familiar with this food, it is allowed as a supplement in the dishes. If you have difficulty getting hold of a certain food or don't want to offer it for any other reason, that's not a problem. Choose an equivalent alternative that your baby likes.

These instructions are not set in stone. The idea is to try something new every day. However, this does not mean that there are not several days on which you offer your baby the same thing. Again, don't let external influences cause unnecessary stress when introducing complementary foods.

The quantities given do not mean that your baby has to eat this amount. Your baby will sometimes eat more and sometimes less. Let's remind ourselves of the basics and the mindset needed to make your baby a happy eater (page 23):

✔ Every child eats differently! Don't set expectations too high and find out how your baby eats by observing.

- ✔ Eating together has many benefits. Be a role model and show your baby all the steps of eating.

- ✔ Ensure a safe and calm environment.

- ✔ Let your baby eat as much or as little as it wants.

- ✔ Always stay relaxed at the dining table.

Ideally, complementary food should be given about 30 minutes to an hour after the last milk meal so that your baby is not too full, but also not too hungry. You should offer a milk meal after the complementary food. This way you continue to provide all the important nutrients. At the same time, digestion is promoted.

You and your baby decide what time of the day to start complementary feeding. Basically, it doesn't matter which meal you start with. It is ideal if the above conditions apply. Start with a meal where the family eats together if possible and which fits in well with your daily routine.

And now: have fun with the introduction of complementary foods!

First week of feeding solids

You will only need very small amounts of food. One or two pieces of finger food or a heaped teaspoon of a meal will probably be enough. It is therefore best to use the ingredients in your own meals so that you don't have to throw too much away. Alternatively, you can freeze the rest for later meals.

It's all about letting your baby explore texture and get to know the taste. Even if your baby only squeezes the food with its hands, sucks on it and then pushes the food out of their mouth again, it's completely normal and already a success. This is because it has just put a food in its mouth for the first time that is not breast/ formula milk. Learning how to eat it is a process of months and even playing with food is a part of it.

There is no specific time of day when it is best to offer complementary food. There are recommendations that say it is best to start complementary foods in the morning or at lunchtime, but this is not a must. Choose a time that works for all of you. Maybe avoid offering a meal with solid food right before nap or bedtime.

Shopping list for week 1

You can buy organic produce, but it is not essential if it is not within your means. In that case, it is only important that you always wash the vegetables thoroughly before preparing them. I would recommend the following foods for the first week of complementary feeding, which you can find in the list below. This list is not fixed. I have included one alternative and of course you are free to add vegetables that are not on the list.

- avocado
- cauliflower
- broccoli
- potato
- pumpkin or squash (alternative)
- parsnip
- spinach
- sweet potatoes (or yams)

Avocado

🕐 **Minutes: 5**   👤 **ready for solids**   🍴 **Portions: 1-2**

❤ **Info:**

Avocado was Ida's first complementary food and she liked it straight away. Ripe avocado has a soft consistency and is easy to suck on. The taste is mild and not too strong. It contains healthy fats, vitamin B, and minerals. It is ideal as a first complementary food, as no further preparation steps are necessary apart from cutting. And it also serves as a nutritious snack later on. You can offer the avocado as puree and finger food at the same time.

🛒 **Ingredients:**

- ✔ ¼ ripe avocado

✏ **Notes:**

👍 **Finger food:**

1. Remove the skin from the avocado and cut off two to three finger-sized pieces.

2. Offer your baby the strips.

🥣 **Puree:**

1. Remove the avocado flesh from the skin and mash with a fork.

2. Offer your baby a few spoons of mashed avocado.

3. If the consistency is too hard, stir 1 tablespoon of hot water into the puree. Then allow the puree to cool to eating temperature.

💡 **Tips:**

✔ The remaining avocado can be stored in the fridge for one to two days and offered again as a complementary food.

✔ Alternatively, the remaining avocado can be used in a salad or guacamole for the grown-ups.

Cauliflower

🕐 **Minutes: 5**
(+ 30 min baking time)

👤 **ready for solids**

🍴 **Portions: 1-2**

❤ **Info:**

Cauliflower has a special flavor that will interest your baby. Similar to broccoli, cauliflower is very suitable as finger food. It contains lots of nutrients and should of course not be missing from the menu.

🛒 **Ingredients:**

- ✔ 3-5 cauliflower florets

✎ **Notes:**

👍 **Finger food:**

1. Wash the cauliflower and cut it so that your baby can easily grasp the stalk.

2. Cook the cauliflower in a steamer for 10 minutes or boil it in a pan of water for 10 minutes.

3. Allow the cauliflower to cool to a safe eating temperature and offer your baby 2 to 3 pieces.

🍲 **Puree:**

1. Wash the cauliflower and cut into small pieces.

2. Cook the cauliflower in a steamer for 10 minutes or boil it in a saucepan of water for 10 minutes.

3. Blend the cooked cauliflower to a puree using a hand blender.

4. Allow the puree to cool down to a safe eating temperature and offer your baby a few spoons with the cauliflower puree.

💡 **Tip:**

- ✔ Not all babies get flatulence from vegetables such as cabbage, garlic, and onions. However, if you are worried about this, start with very small amounts and observe whether your baby develops intestinal problems.

Potato

⏲ **Minutes: 15**   👤 **ready for solids**   🍴 **Portions: 1-2**

💜 **Info:**

Potatoes are healthy because they contain important nutrients and fiber that are good for digestion. They also have a mild taste, can be prepared in a variety of ways and have the perfect consistency for finger food when cooked. Serve the potato without the skin, as your baby is not yet able to crush it well.

🛒 **Ingredients:**

   ✔ 1 potato

✏ **Notes:**

👍 **Finger food:**

1. Peel the potato and cut into finger-sized pieces.

2. Cook the potato pieces in a steamer for 10 minutes or boil them in a pan of water for 10 minutes.

3. Allow the potato pieces to cool to a safe eating temperature and offer your baby 2 to 3 pieces.

🥣 **Puree:**

1. Peel the potato and cut into small pieces.

2. Cook the potato pieces in a steamer for 10 minutes or boil them in a saucepan with water for 10 minutes.

3. Mash the cooked potato pieces with a hand blender.

4. Allow the puree to cool to a safe eating temperature and offer your baby a few spoons thereof.

💡 **Tips:**

✔ For a more liquid consistency, a little cooking water or breast/formula milk can be added.

✔ Offer a few spoonful's of mashed potato as well as one or two pieces of potato to try out. This promotes your baby's motor skills.

Parsnip

🕐 **Minutes: 15**　　　👤 **ready for solids**　　　🍴 **Portions: 1-2**

❤ **Info:**

Parsnips are a mild, sweet root vegetable that contains many nutrients. They are an autumn and winter vegetable, but are still available longer if stored well. Parsnip is one of the classic baby food recipes and comes in finger food form.

🛒 **Ingredients:**

- ✔ 1 parsnip

✏ **Notes:**

👍 Finger food:

1. Peel the parsnip and cut into finger-sized pieces.

2. Cook the parsnip in a steamer for 10 minutes or boil in a pan of water for 10 minutes.

3. Allow the parsnip to cool to a safe eating temperature and offer your baby 2 to 3 pieces.

🥣 Puree:

1. Peel the parsnip and cut into small pieces.

2. Cook the parsnip in a steamer for 10 minutes or boil in a small pot of water for 10 minutes.

3. Blend the cooked parsnip into a mash using a hand blender.

4. Allow the puree to cool to a safe eating temperature and offer your baby a few spoons full.

💡 Tips:

- Parsnips and other root vegetables make wonderful finger food and puree.

- If all food was previously only offered as finger food, this is a nice opportunity for your baby to now get to know a spoon and explore its functions.

Sweet potato

🕐 **Minutes: 15**   👤 **ready for solids**   🍴 **Portions: 1-2**

❤ **Info:**

Sweet potatoes, also known as yams, are much like potatoes, only sweet and mostly orange in color. They can be boiled, steamed, baked, roasted or deep-fried. Many children prefer them because of their sweet taste. They are often available in restaurants as an alternative to conventional potato fries and can also be ordered unsalted. This unsalted version is ideal as a complementary food.

🛒 **Ingredients:**

- ✔ 1 small sweet potato

✏ **Notes:**

👍 Finger food:

1. Peel the sweet potato and cut into finger-sized pieces.

2. Cook the sweet potato in a steamer for 8 minutes or boil it in a small pot of water for 8 minutes.

3. Allow the sweet potato to cool to a safe eating temperature and offer your baby 2 to 3 pieces.

🥣 Puree:

1. Peel the sweet potato and cut into small pieces.

2. Cook the sweet potato in a steamer for 8 minutes or boil it in a pan of water for 8 minutes.

3. Blend the cooked sweet potato into a puree using a hand blender.

4. Allow the puree to cool to a safe eating temperature and offer your baby a few spoonful's of the sweet potato puree.

💡 Tip:

- ✔ You can also make a family meal with sweet potatoes. I recommend sweet potato fries from the oven. Preheat the oven to200 °C thermos fan (220 °C F top/bottom heat). Peel the sweet potato and cut it into wedges. Place the sweet potato sticks on a baking tray lined with baking paper and bake for 20 minutes. For older eaters, you can season the fries as required after baking.

Broccoli

🕐 **Minutes: 15**   👤 **ready for solids**   🍴 **Portions: 1-2**

❤ **Info:**

Broccoli is not the most popular vegetable with children, but by getting to know it early and offering it regularly, this does not necessarily have to be the case. Broccoli is a versatile vegetable that is particularly interesting for babies. The smooth stalk and small buds provide a great texture in the hand and mouth. It's one of Ida's favorite vegetables, which she requests regularly.

🛒 **Ingredients:**

- ✔ 3-5 broccoli florets

✏ **Notes:**

👍 **Finger food:**

1. Wash the broccoli and cut it so that your baby can easily grasp the stalk.

2. Cook the broccoli in a steamer for 10 minutes or boil it in a saucepan with water for 10 minutes.

3. Allow the broccoli to cool to a safe eating temperature and offer your baby 2 to 3 pieces.

🥣 **Puree:**

1. Wash the broccoli and cut into small pieces.

2. Cook the broccoli in a steamer for 10 minutes or boil it in a saucepan with water for 10 minutes.

3. Blend the cooked broccoli with a hand blender.

4. Allow the puree to cool to a safe eating temperature and offer your baby a few spoons of the broccoli puree.

💡 **Tip:**

✔ The remaining broccoli can be frozen both in finger food and puree form. The puree can be pre-portioned in an ice cube tray, for example.

Spinach

🕐 **Minutes: 10**   👤 **ready for solids**   🍴 **Portions: 1-2**

❤ **Info:**

Spinach on the seventh day of complementary feeding is a perfect idea, because the earlier and more often you introduce your baby to bitter-tasting foods, the more likely it is that it will continue to like them in the future. Fresh, raw spinach leaves are not suitable as finger food as they can stick to the roof of the mouth. I therefore recommend only offering spinach cooked and chopped or pureed.

🛒 **Ingredients:**

- ✔ 1 handful of fresh spinach or 3 pieces of chopped frozen spinach (plain)
- ✔ 2-3 pieces of vegetables prepared on the previous days

✏ **Notes:**

👍 **Finger food:**

1. Wash the fresh spinach and place in a bowl. Bring water to the boil in a kettle, pour over the spinach and leave to infuse for 2 minutes. Alternatively, prepare the (plain) frozen spinach according to the packet instructions.

2. Heat the other vegetables to eating temperature.

3. Finely chop the cooked spinach with a knife.

4. Allow the spinach to cool to a safe eating temperature and offer it to your baby as a dip with 2 to 3 pieces of vegetables.

🥣 **Puree:**

1. Wash the fresh spinach and place in a bowl. Bring the water to the boil in a kettle, pour over the spinach and leave to infuse for 2 minutes. Alternatively, prepare the (plain) frozen spinach according to the packet instructions.

2. Heat the vegetables to eating temperature.

3. Blend all the ingredients with a hand blender.

4. Allow the puree to cool to a safe eating temperature and offer a few spoons thereof to your baby.

💡 **Tip:**

✔ Chopped spinach with pasta can be offered as an idea for future complementary food recipes. Spiralized pasta (fusilli) is ideal for babies to grab.

Pumpkin

🕐 **Minutes: 15**   👤 **ready for solids**   🍴 **Portions: 1-2**

♥ **Info:**

My girls loved pumpkin, also known as butternut or squash, right from the start. Due to its creamy and not too firm consistency and its sweet taste, it is ideal as a first complementary food. Pumpkin is also available beyond the fall months because it has a good shelf life.

🛒 **Ingredients:**

- ✔ 1 hand-sized piece of pumpkin

✏ **Notes:**

👍 **Finger food:**

1. Wash the pumpkin, remove the seeds and skin and cut into finger-sized pieces.

2. Cook the pumpkin in a steamer for 8 minutes or boil it in a small pot of water for 8 minutes.

3. Allow the pumpkin to cool to a safe eating temperature and offer your baby 2 to 3 pieces.

🥣 **Puree:**

1. Wash the pumpkin, remove the seeds and skin and cut into small pieces.

2. Cook the pumpkin in a steamer for 8 minutes or boil it in a small pot of water for 8 minutes.

3. Blend the cooked pumpkin to a puree using a hand blender.

4. Allow the puree to cool to a safe eating temperature and offer your baby a few spoons thereof.

💡 **Tips:**

- The remaining pumpkin can be used to make pumpkin soup for the rest of the family.

- The remaining finger food pumpkin can be used in a salad for mature eaters.

Second week of feeding solids

How did the first week of offering solids to your baby go? Did you have fun? If your baby's reaction to solids is still cautious, don't let this put you off. Stay patient and give your baby time to explore and try things out.

In the second week of introducing complementary foods, we will offer some familiar foods as well as trying out new foods. Meals will become more complex, iron-rich foods and a few allergens will be added. After all, allergens are best introduced under the protection of breast milk. If your baby gets infant formula, this is of course no problem either.

Once you have settled in a little, you can try to make mealtimes a routine. Try to stick to a regular mealtime that works well for you and your baby. If this doesn't work out, it's no big deal. Life happens and your baby doesn't work like an alarm clock. So, don't put any pressure on yourself, routines will come automatically over time.

Stay relaxed and don't expect your baby to learn to eat more quickly. It's still just about learning all the skills necessary for eating by themselves and not about getting your baby filled up with solid food. Breast/formula milk remains the most important source of nutrition for optimal nutrient supply and should continue to be offered as usual.

Puree and finger food

If you preferred to offer puree in the first week, you could be brave and play with new textures a little and no longer puree the food finely, but only mash it. Observe how your baby reacts to this. Be bold and trust your baby. The gag reflex naturally protects your baby from choking. Just observe your baby and it will show you what it likes.

Shopping list for week 2

The following shopping list is not fixed but is intended to show you which foods are baby-friendly. You can swap foods or leave them out if they don't suit your eating style. You can replace fresh food with frozen food. Just make sure that everything is sufficiently cooked and soft enough. It remains important that you offer as wide a variety of foods as possible.

- Avocado
- Organic eggs
- Organic minced beef
- Broccoli
- Cherry tomatoes
- Green beans
- Chicken breast fillet
- Potato
- Chickpeas (tin or jar)
- Almond butter (100 % almonds, without salt)
- Parsnip
- Red lentils (dried)
- Spinach
- Sweet potato

Sweet potatoes and red lentils

🕐 **Minutes: 15**   👤 **ready for solids**   🍴 **Portions: 1-2**

❤ **Info:**

Your baby already knows sweet potatoes from the first week. Today we want to offer them in combination with red lentils. All types of lentils are an excellent vegetarian source of iron. They are also high in fiber, which will have a positive effect on your baby's digestion. You don't necessarily have to use red lentils, you can also use other varieties. The only important thing is that they do not contain any salt or other additives.

🛒 **Ingredients:**

- ✔ 1 small sweet potato
- ✔ 2 tsp red lentils (dried)

✏ **Notes:**

👍 **Finger food:**

1. Peel the sweet potato and cut into finger-sized pieces.

2. Cook the sweet potato pieces in a steamer for 8 minutes or boil them in a pan of water for 8 minutes.

3. Prepare the lentils according to the packet instructions.

4. Roll the sweet potato pieces in the cooked lentils, leave to cool to a safe eating temperature and offer your baby 2 to 3 pieces.

🥣 **Puree:**

1. Peel the sweet potato and cut into small pieces.

2. Cook the sweet potato pieces in a steamer for 8 minutes or boil them in a pan of water for 8 minutes.

3. Prepare the lentils according to the packet instructions.

4. Blend the sweet potato chunks and lentils with a hand blender until smooth.

5. Allow the puree to cool to a safe eating temperature and offer your baby a few spoons full.

💡 **Tip:**

✔ Lentils and sweet potato can be used to make a soup for the rest of the family. To do this, sauté chopped onions in a pan with oil, add cooked lentils and sweet potato to the pan, cover with water and bring to the boil. Add 2 tablespoons of cream and blend everything to a soup using a hand blender. Season with salt and pepper.

Spinach and egg

🕐 **Minutes: 15**   👤 **ready for solids**   🍴 **Portions: 1-2**

❤ **Info:**

Creamed spinach with mashed potatoes and egg is a classic dish from my childhood and probably that of many other parents too. In a modified form, it is the perfect dish for introducing complementary foods. Egg contains lots of protein and iron. You should generally be cautious with protein in the first year. Excessive consumption can put a strain on the baby's kidneys. However, one or two eggs a week are safe. Be aware that egg is an allergen.

🛒 **Ingredients:**

- ✔ 1 organic egg

- ✔ 1 handful of fresh spinach or 3 pieces of chopped frozen spinach (plain)

✎ **Notes:**

👍 **Finger food:**

1. Boil the egg in a saucepan with water for 10 minutes. Then rinse with cold water, remove the shell and cut the egg into quarters.

2. Wash the fresh spinach and place in a bowl. Bring the water to the boil in a kettle, pour over the spinach and leave to infuse for 2 minutes. Alternatively, prepare the (plain) frozen spinach according to the packet instructions.

3. Finely chop the cooked spinach with a knife.

4. Pour the spinach over two egg quarters, leave to cool to a safe eating temperature and offer to your baby.

🥣 **Puree:**

1. Boil the egg in a pan of water for 10 minutes. Then rinse with cold water, remove the shell and roughly chop the egg.

2. Wash the fresh spinach and place in a bowl. Bring the water to the boil in a kettle, pour over the spinach and leave to infuse for 2 minutes. Alternatively, prepare the frozen (plain) spinach according to the packet instructions.

3. Blend all the ingredients together with a hand blender.

4. Allow the puree to cool to a safe eating temperature and offer your baby a few spoons full.

💡 **Tip:**

✔ Eggs must always be fully cooked for babies and should never be offered raw or half-raw due to the risk of salmonella.

Broccoli and potato

🕐 **Minutes: 15**   👤 **ready for solids**   🍴 **Portions: 1-2**

❤ **Info:**

Broccoli and potatoes are a perfect combination and your baby will probably already be familiar with them from the first week of complementary feeding. Potatoes are mild and have a soft consistency, broccoli has a slightly stronger taste and a grainy texture. If you still have frozen vegetables left over from the first week, you can use them for this complementary food meal.

🛒 **Ingredients:**

- ✔ 1 potato

- ✔ 3 broccoli florets

✎ **Notes:**

👍 **Finger food:**

1. Peel the potato, wash the broccoli and cut everything into finger-sized pieces.

2. Cook the potato and broccoli in a steamer for 10 minutes or boil in a pan of water for 10 minutes.

3. Allow the potato and broccoli to cool to a safe eating temperature and offer your baby 2 to 3 pieces of each.

🥣 **Puree:**

1. Peel the potato, wash the broccoli and cut everything into finger-sized pieces.

2. Cook the potato and broccoli in a steamer for 10 minutes or boil in a saucepan with water for 10 minutes.

3. Blend the ingredients with a hand blender.

4. Allow the puree to cool to a safe eating temperature and offer a spoonful or two to your baby.

💡 **Tip:**

✔ If you are not yet confident enough to offer finger food, you can also shape the vegetable mash into small finger food rolls, bake in the oven for 10 minutes at 200 °C (220 °C top/bottom heat) and serve. The consistency of the puree should not be too runny.

Avocado and almond butter

🕐 **Minutes: 5**   👤 **ready for solids**   🍴 **Portions: 1-2**

❤ **Info:**

Nut butters are ideal for starting complementary foods as they contain lots of valuable nutrients and healthy fats. Nuts are an allergen but should not be missing from the complementary food menu as they are high in calories, and can thus be used to enrich low-calorie dishes. It is important that the nut butter consists of 100% nuts and does not contain any additional salt.

🛒 **Ingredients:**

- ✔ ¼ ripe avocado
- ✔ 1 tsp almond butter

✏ **Notes:**

👍 **Finger food:**

1. Remove the skin from the avocado quarter and cut two to three finger-sized pieces from the flesh.

2. Spread the avocado pieces with almond butter and offer them to your baby.

🥣 **Puree:**

1. Remove the flesh of the avocado from the skin and mash with a fork.

2. Add the almond butter to the mashed avocado, mix thoroughly and offer a spoonful or two to your baby.

💡 **Tip:**

✔ Nut butter is a good source of iron and can be perfectly combined with fruit. The vitamin C from the fruit ensures optimal utilization of the iron still bound in the body.

Green beans and chicken

⏱ **Minutes: 15**   👤 **ready for solids**   🍴 **Portions: 1-2**

❤ **Info:**

Today is your baby's first meal with meat. But no need to worry. Even without teeth, babies can eat meat - by chewing on it, sucking it out and then leaving the meat fibers on the plate. Green beans are a perfect finger food vegetable when cooked, as they already have the right shape.

🛒 **Ingredients:**

- ✔ 50 g green beans
- ✔ 50 g chicken breast fillet

✎ **Notes:**

👍 **Finger food:**

1. Wash the beans and cut off the ends.

2. Wash the chicken breast, pat dry, and cut into finger-sized pieces.

3. Cook the beans and chicken in a steamer for 10 minutes or boil in a pan of water for 10 minutes.

4. Then, remove the inner peas from the beans, mash them and spread them over the chicken.

5. Allow the chicken and beans to cool to a safe eating temperature and offer your baby 2 to 3 pieces at a time.

🥣 **Puree:**

1. Wash the beans and cut off the ends.

2. Wash the chicken breast, pat dry, and cut into pieces.

3. Cook the beans and chicken in a steamer for 10 minutes or boil in a pan of water for 10 minutes.

4. Blend all the ingredients with a hand blender.

5. Allow the puree to cool to a safe eating temperature and offer your baby a few bites.

💡 **Tips:**

- Turkey breast is also suitable as an alternative to chicken breast. The preparation remains the same.

- The meat of the chicken leg contains the most iron.

Tomatoes and chickpeas

Minutes: 15 **ready for solids** **Portions: 1-2**

Info:

Many children don't like tomatoes. This is often the case because they usually get introduced into their diet at a very late stage. They are an excellent source of vitamins and antioxidants. Chickpeas are a good source of iron, but in their natural shape they pose a high risk of choking. That's why they are mashed in today's recipe.

Ingredients:

- 5 cherry tomatoes
- 30 g chickpeas (tin or glass jar)

Notes:

👍 **Finger food:**

1. Wash the tomatoes and cut into quarters.

2. Remove the chickpeas from the tin or jar and drain.

3. Cook the tomatoes and chickpeas in a steamer for 5 minutes.

4. Mash the chickpeas with a fork and spread over the tomatoes.

5. Allow the tomatoes and chickpeas to cool to a safe eating temperature and offer them to your baby.

🥣 **Puree:**

1. Wash the tomatoes and cut into quarters.

2. Remove the chickpeas from the tin and drain.

3. Cook the tomatoes and chickpeas in a steamer for 5 minutes.

4. Peel the tomatoes and blend with the chickpeas using a hand blender.

5. Allow the puree to cool to a safe eating temperature and offer a spoonful or two to your baby.

💡 **Tips:**

- Raw, tomatoes are generally suitable as finger food but are one of the most plump foods and should therefore always be cut into at least quarters.

- Raw tomatoes can sometimes cause skin irritation around the mouth. This is usually not an allergy, but a temporary skin irritation.

Parsnip and beef

🕐 **Minutes: 20**   👤 **ready for solids**   🍴 **Portions: 1-2**

❤ **Info:**

Beef is a very good source of iron. As the iron in meat is not bound, it is particularly easy for the body to utilize. It therefore makes sense to introduce it early if you eat beef. Other types of meat are also possible. In combination with parsnip, the dish becomes slightly sweet.

🛒 **Ingredients:**

- ✔ 1 parsnip
- ✔ 100 g organic minced beef

✏ **Notes:**

👍 **Finger food:**

1. Peel the parsnip and cut into finger-sized pieces.

2. Cook the parsnip in a steamer for 10 minutes and then blend one half with a hand blender to a puree.

3. Mix the parsnip puree into the beef, shape into teaspoon-sized oval meatballs with clean hands and cook in a steamer for 10 minutes.

4. Allow the remaining parsnip pieces and the meatballs to cool to a safe eating temperature and offer them to your baby.

🥣 **Puree:**

1. Peel the parsnip and cut into finger-sized pieces.

2. Divide the minced meat into large, flat pieces with your hands.

3. Cook the parsnip and meat in a steamer for 10 minutes.

4. Blend the cooked ingredients with a hand blender to make puree, leave to cool to a safe eating temperature and offer your baby a few bites.

💡 **Tip:**

✔ The meat mash can be served as a dip for vegetable finger food.

Third week of feeding solids

You now have two exciting weeks of complementary feeding behind you. Your baby may have already understood what the new food is all about, or may still be playing with it most of the time. Don't stress yourselves and stick to the routine. If you feel that you still need a little more time, repeat the second week of complementary feeding. There is no need to rush.

If you haven't already done so, now is a good time to give your baby a spoon with every meal. Support your baby by filling the spoon with food and place it in a position ready to pick up. Your baby is sure to mirror what you do with your cutlery. In this way, you are already encouraging independent eating with cutlery.

In this third week we want to focus on spices, as early introduction can help to avoid picky eating later. The spices will give your baby a new and interesting flavor to discover.

Shopping list for week 3

As in previous weeks, the same applies to the shopping list: You can swap out foods that don't fit in with your family meal plan at any time.

- ✔ Eggplant
- ✔ Organic egg
- ✔ Organic minced beef
- ✔ Peas
- ✔ Chicken breast fillet
- ✔ Pumpkin or squash
- ✔ Ginger
- ✔ Cod fillet
- ✔ Carrot
- ✔ Potato
- ✔ Lentils
- ✔ Mild curry powder
- ✔ Bell peppers
- ✔ Parsley
- ✔ Rice
- ✔ Red onion
- ✔ Zucchini

Pumpkin, carrot and ginger

🕐 **Minutes: 15**   👤 **ready for solids**   🍴 **Portions: 1-2**

❤ **Info:**

Pumpkin and carrots are ideal as finger food or puree due to their consistency. They also contain valuable nutrients, have a slightly sweet taste and are generally well received by children. Ginger has an exciting taste and has a particularly positive effect on the digestive system.

🛒 **Ingredients:**

- ✔ 50 g pumpkin or butternut squash
- ✔ 50 g organic carrots
- ✔ 1 pinch of freshly grated ginger

✎ **Notes:**

👍 **Finger food:**

1. Peel the carrots and pumpkin, remove the seeds from the pumpkin and cut the carrots and pumpkin into finger-sized pieces.

2. Cook the vegetables in a steamer for 10 minutes.

3. Blend half of the carrots and half of the pumpkin with a hand blender and mix with a pinch of freshly grated ginger.

4. Allow everything to cool to a safe eating temperature and offer your baby the vegetable pieces with the carrot-pumpkin-ginger mash as a dip.

🥣 **Puree:**

1. Peel the carrots and pumpkin, remove the seeds from the pumpkin and cut the carrots and pumpkin into small pieces.

2. Cook the vegetables in a steamer for 10 minutes.

3. Blend the carrots and pumpkin with a pinch of freshly grated ginger, using a hand blender.

4. Allow the puree to cool to a safe eating temperature and offer your baby a few bites.

💡 **Tip:**

✔ Ginger is slightly spicy, so only a pinch of freshly grated ginger is enough.

Peas, fish and rice

 Minutes: 20   ready for solids   Portions: 1-2

♥ Info:

Fish provides easily digestible, high-quality protein and omega-3 fatty acids. It is also an allergen. That is why it is already on the menu today. With peas as a vegetable and rice as a high-calorie food, this dish is particularly balanced.

🛒 Ingredients:

- ✔ 30 g jasmin rice
- ✔ 50 g cod fillet
- ✔ 1 tbsp frozen peas

✏ Notes:

👍 **Finger food:**

1. Prepare the rice according to the packet instructions until is soft and sticky.

2. Cook the peas and fish fillet in a steamer for 10 minutes.

3. Mash all the peas with a fork to prevent choking and then mix them with the rice. Form oval shaped finger-food pieces.

4. Allow the pea rice and fish to cool to a safe eating temperature and offer to your baby.

🥣 **Puree:**

1. Prepare the rice according to the packet instructions.

2. Cook the peas and fish fillet in a steamer for 10 minutes.

3. Blend the peas, rice and fish with a hand blender until smooth.

4. Allow the puree to cool to a safe eating temperature and offer a spoonful or two to your baby.

💡 **Tip:**

✔ When it comes to fish, cod is a good choice because it can only be caught wild and not farmed. In contrast to farmed and freshwater fish, wild-caught fish from the sea is less contaminated with harmful substances.

Bell peppers, zucchinis and onions

⏲ **Minutes: 15**   👤 **ready for solids**   🍴 **Portions: 1-2**

❤ **Info:**

Many parents are concerned that onions and garlic could give their baby a stomach ache. However, this cannot be generalized. That's why I recommend testing this early on so as not to deprive your baby of something based on false assumptions. The bell peppers and zucchinis have a slightly bitter note, while the onion rounds off the dish with its slight sweetness when cooked.

🛒 **Ingredients:**

- ✔ ¼ red onion
- ✔ ½ small zucchini
- ✔ ½ bell pepper (red or yellow)

✎ **Notes:**

👍 **Finger food:**

1. Peel the onion and cut into half-moon slices.

2. Wash the bell peppers and zucchinis, cut into finger-sized pieces and cook together with the onions in a steamer for 8 minutes.

3. Allow the ingredients to cool to a safe eating temperature and offer to your baby.

4. If you still have some of the carrot-pumpkin-ginger puree from week 3 day 1 (page 104) left, you can also offer this.

🍲 **Puree:**

1. Peel the onion and cut into small pieces.

2. Wash the bell peppers and zucchinis, cut into small pieces and cook together with the onion pieces in a steamer for 8 minutes.

3. Blend the ingredients with a hand blender.

4. Allow the puree to cool to a safe eating temperature and offer your baby a few bites.

💡 **Tip:**

✔ The vegetable sticks keep for two to three days in the fridge and are also suitable for on the go.

Eggplant, lentils and parsley

🕐 **Minutes: 15**　　　👤 **ready for solids**　　　🍴 **Portions: 1-2**

💜 **Info:**

On todays menu is eggplant, with lentils as a vegetarian source of iron. To get your baby used to herbs in food, parsley is a good start due to its mild flavor.

🛒 **Ingredients:**

- ✔ 1 thick slice of eggplant
- ✔ 30 g lentils
- ✔ 5 leaves of fresh parsley

✏ **Notes:**

👍 **Finger food:**

1. Cut the eggplant slice into 1 cm thick strips and cook in a steamer for 5 minutes.

2. Cook the lentils according to the packet instructions until very soft.

3. Finely chop the parsley, mix into the cooked lentils and pour over the eggplants.

4. Allow the ingredients to cool to a safe eating temperature and offer to your baby.

🥣 **Puree:**

1. Cut the eggplant slice into small pieces and cook in a steamer for 5 minutes.

2. Cook the lentils according to the packet instructions.

3. Finely chop the parsley.

4. Blend all the ingredients together with a hand blender.

5. Allow the puree to cool to a safe eating temperature and offer your baby a few bites.

💡 **Tip:**

- The more often you mix food with green herbs and fresh spices, the more normal this will be for your baby. This will help you avoid later complaints such as "Eww, there's something green on my plate!"

Potatoes, egg and broccoli

⏱ **Minutes: 15**　　　👤 **ready for solids**　　　🍴 **Portions: 1-2**

❤ **Info:**

We are slowly working towards a balanced baby plate. Ideally, this should always consist of a source of calories, a source of iron and a source of vitamins. So today we have potatoes as a source of calories, eggs as a source of iron and broccoli as a source of vitamins.

🛒 **Ingredients:**

- ✔ 1 potato
- ✔ 1 organic egg
- ✔ 5 broccoli florets

✏ **Notes:**

👍 **Finger food:**

1. Peel the potato, wash the broccoli and cut everything into finger-sized pieces.

2. Cook the potatoes and broccoli in a steamer for 10 minutes or in a saucepan with water for 10 minutes.

3. Boil the egg in a small pot of water for 10 minutes. Then rinse with cold water, remove the shell and cut into quarters.

4. Allow the ingredients to cool to a safe eating temperature and offer to your baby.

🥣 **Pure:**

1. Peel the potato, wash the broccoli and cut everything into small pieces.

2. Steam the potatoes and broccoli in a steamer for 10 minutes or boil them in a pan of water for 10 minutes.

3. Boil the egg in a pan of water for 10 minutes. Then rinse and remove the shell.

4. Blend all the ingredients together with a hand blender.

5. Allow the puree to cool to a safe eating temperature and offer your baby a few bites.

💡 **Tip:**

- If you have any parsley left over, you can use it when finely chopped in this recipe.

Curried sweet potato and chicken

🕐 **Minutes: 15**   👤 **ready for solids**   🍴 **Portions: 1-2**

❤ **Info:**

Curry sounds exotic and too spicy, but you can find mild curry powder in almost any supermarket and create a great taste experience for your baby. The chicken is a good source of iron, and the sweet potato is a healthy vegetable with a sweet taste.

🛒 **Ingredients:**

- ✔ 70 g sweet potato
- ✔ 50 g chicken breast fillet
- ✔ 1 pinch of mild curry powder

✏ **Notes:**

👍 **Finger food:**

1. Peel the sweet potato, rinse and pat the chicken dry. Then cut everything into finger-sized pieces.

2. Steam the sweet potato and chicken in a steamer for 10 minutes or boil in a pan of water for 10 minutes.

3. Sprinkle the curry powder over the sweet potatoes and chicken strips, allow everything to cool to a safe eating temperature and offer to your baby.

🥣 **Puree:**

1. Peel the sweet potato, rinse and pat the chicken dry. Then cut everything into finger-sized pieces.

2. Cook the sweet potato and chicken in a steamer for 10 minutes or in a saucepan with water for 10 minutes.

3. Blend all the ingredients together with a hand blender.

4. Allow the puree to cool to a safe eating temperature and offer your baby a few spoons full.

💡 **Tip:**

- Finely chopped fresh coriander is a great flavorful and, above all, green addition.

Beef with vegetables and herbs

🕐 **Minutes: 20**   👤 **ready for solids**   🍴 **Portions: 1-2**

❤ **Info:**

On the last day of the third week, you can reuse the leftovers from the previous days. The remaining vegetables and minced beef make wonderful meatballs. Your baby is sure to enjoy dipping them in the week's leftover dip.

🛒 **Ingredients:**

- ✔ 100 g cooked vegetables (leftovers from the week)

- ✔ 100 g organic minced beef

- ✔ Herbs (leftovers of the week)

✏ **Notes:**

👍 **Finger food:**

1. Either use the remaining vegetables and herbs from the previous days or prepare the vegetables and herbs freshly as described in the previous recipes.

2. Mash the cooked vegetables and herbs in a bowl with a fork.

3. Add the minced beef, shape it into teaspoon-sized, oblong meatballs with clean hands and steam in a steamer for 10 minutes.

4. Allow the meatballs to cool to a safe eating temperature and offer them to your baby. If you have any dips left, you can serve these with them.

🍲 **Puree:**

1. Either use the remaining vegetables and herbs from the previous days or prepare the vegetables and herbs freshly as described in the previous recipes.

2. Shape the minced beef into coarse, flat pieces with clean hands and cook in a steamer for 10 minutes.

3. Blend all the ingredients together with a hand blender.

4. Allow the puree to cool to a safe eating temperature and offer a few bites to your baby.

💡 **Tip:**

✔ The type of meat can be substituted. This means you can prepare different variations of meatballs.

Fourth week of feeding solids

You may have noticed that there have been no processed foods in the recipes so far. Processed foods, such as dairy products and baked goods, usually contain ingredients such as salt, sugar or similar. That's why we have completely avoided them.

You've probably also noticed that no fruit has been on the shopping list up to this point and the focus has been more on vegetables. This week we want to try these things too, so that you can get an even better feel for what is possible with complementary foods in this early stage.

More meals

If you have the feeling that your baby wants to eat more often, you can introduce more meals now. Offer something baby-friendly from your plate or give your baby the leftovers from the previous day, together with a new meal. However, it is also fine to introduce another meal every four to six weeks.

Stay relaxed and don't expect your baby to learn to eat very quickly. It's still about learning all the eating skills and not about getting your baby full. Breast/ formula milk remains the most important source of nutrition for optimal nutrient supply and should be offered as usual.

If your baby is still eating cautiously, there is no reason not to repeat the meals of the previous weeks and wait a little longer before going to the next phase.

Shopping list for week 4

As in previous weeks, you can swap out ingredients in this food list that don't fit your diet. The meals will be a little more complex and are already very similar to what the rest of the family would eat.

- Apple
- Banana
- Basil
- Organic egg
- Organic minced beef
- Organic blueberries (alternatively strawberries)
- Spelt flour
- Soft oats (not rolled or steel-cut)
- Spring onions
- Green asparagus (alternatively pumpkin or squash)
- Chicken breast fillet
- Chickpeas (tin or jar)
- Kidney beans (tin or jar)
- Dairy or plant-based milk
- Almond butter
- Mozzarella
- Oregano
- Bell pepper
- Round (short) grain rice
- Spinach (fresh or frozen)
- Sweet potato
- Tomatoes
- Thyme
- Whole-wheat pasta
- Wild salmon
- Lemon

Banana three ways

⏱ **Minutes: 5** 👤 **ready for solids** 🍴 **Portions: 1-2**

❤ **Info:**

Bananas are true all-rounders. They are a particularly energy-rich fruit and can be used wonderfully in various dishes or enjoyed as a snack between meals. To add even more nutrients, bananas can be perfectly complemented with iron-rich oats and nut butter as a healthy fatty acid.

🛒 **Ingredients:**

- ✔ ½ banana
- ✔ 1 tsp baby oats
- ✔ 1 tsp almond butter

✎ **Notes:**

👍 **Finger food:**

1. Peel half the banana and cut or divide into three pieces.

2. Roll a piece of banana in oat flakes.

3. Spread another piece of banana with almond butter.

4. Leave the last piece of banana without toppings.

5. Offer your baby all three banana varieties.

🥣 **Puree:**

1. Peel half the banana and mash it with a fork.

2. Mix both the rolled oats and the almond butter into the banana puree and stir thoroughly.

3. Offer your baby a few spoons of the mix.

💡 **Tip:**

✔ Bananas have a varying effect on digestion. Very ripe bananas can have a laxative effect, while unripe bananas can have a constipating effect.

Tomato and mozzarella with basil

🕐 **Minutes: 5**   👤 **ready for solids**   🍴 **Portions: 1-2**

❤ **Info:**

Today is the first time we offer a dairy product. Mozzarella is ideal as finger food for babies. It contains little salt and has a baby-friendly consistency. Basil is a mild but interesting herb that you should not deprive your baby of.

🛒 **Ingredients:**

- ✔ 1 tomato

- ✔ ¼ mozzarella ball
  (from pasteurized milk)

- ✔ 2 basil leaves

✏ **Notes:**

👍 **Finger food:**

1. Wash the tomato thoroughly, halve and cut into 1 cm thick slices.

2. Drain the mozzarella and cut into 1 cm thick slices.

3. Wash and finely chop the basil.

4. Roll the tomato and mozzarella slices in the basil and offer them to your baby.

🥣 **Puree:**

1. Wash the tomato and cut into small pieces.

2. Drain the mozzarella and cut into small pieces.

3. Wash the basil and blend with the tomatoes and mozzarella using a hand blender.

4. Offer your baby a few bites.

💡 **Tips:**

- ✔ Cherry tomatoes are also suitable for complementary feeding, but they should be offered at least quartered.

- ✔ Your baby will usually simply spit out the tomato peel that it cannot swallow. This means you don't need to peel the tomato in advance or be worried about whether your baby can eat the tomato skin.

Pasta with spinach and salmon

🕐 **Minutes: 15**   👤 **ready for solids**   🍴 **Portions: 1-2**

❤ **Info:**

Whole-wheat pasta tastes good to most babies straight away. In my experience, spiralized noodles (fusilli) offer the best grip for baby's hands. The combination of carbohydrates, fiber, protein, iron and other nutrients is ideal for baby's meal.

🛒 **Ingredients:**

- ✔ 20 g whole-wheat pasta
- ✔ 1 handful of fresh spinach or 3 pieces of chopped frozen spinach (without additives)
- ✔ 60 g wild salmon

✎ **Notes:**

👍 Finger food:

1. Prepare the pasta according to the packet instructions.

2. Cook the wild salmon in a steamer for 10 minutes.

3. Wash the fresh spinach and place in a bowl. Bring the water to the boil in a kettle, pour over the spinach and leave it for 2 minutes. Alternatively, prepare the frozen spinach according to the packet instructions.

4. Finely chop the cooked spinach with a knife.

5. Allow the salmon, pasta and spinach to cool to a safe eating temperature and offer to your baby.

🥣 Puree:

1. Prepare the pasta according to the packet instructions.

2. Cook the wild salmon in a steamer for 10 minutes.

3. Wash the fresh spinach and place in a bowl. Bring the water to the boil in a kettle, pour over the spinach and leave it for 2 minutes. Alternatively, prepare the frozen spinach according to the packet instructions.

4. Finely chop the cooked spinach with a knife.

5. Blend all the ingredients together with a hand blender and allow to cool to a safe eating temperature.

6. Offer a few spoons full to your baby.

💡 Tip:

- ✔ As an alternative to fish, you could sprinkle some grated mozzarella over the pasta or blend it into the puree.

Muesli and berries

🕐 **Minutes: 15**   👤 **ready for solids**   🍴 **Portions: 1-2**

❤️ **Info:**

Whole blueberries pose a risk of chocking due to their plump shape. Crushed or cut into small pieces, however, they are safe to offer.

🛒 **Ingredients:**

- ✔ 1 tbsp oats
- ✔ 4 tbsp milk (plant-based milk)
- ✔ ½ tsp nut butter of your choice
- ✔ ¼ apple
- ✔ 5 blueberries

✏️ **Notes:**

👍 Finger food:

1. Heat the milk gently in a pan. Stir in the oats and nut butter and pour into a bowl.

2. Wash the apple and grate finely with a grater.

3. Wash and cut the blueberries.

4. Mix the apple and blueberries into the oats.

5. Allow the muesli to cool to eating temperature and offer it to your baby. It can be eaten with a baby-hand friendly spoon or without.

🥣 Puree:

1. Heat the milk gently in a pan. Stir in the rolled oats and nut butter and pour into a bowl.

2. Wash the apple and grate finely with a grater.

3. Wash and quarter the blueberries.

4. Add the apple and blueberries to the oats and blend with a hand blender until smooth.

5. Allow the puree to cool to eating temperature and offer your baby a few bites.

💡 Tip:

- Blueberries are a low-fructose source of vitamins and therefore an ideal snack between meals.

Rice with green asparagus and chicken

🕐 **Minutes: 20**   👤 **ready for solids**   🍴 **Portions: 1-2**

❤ **Info:**

This dish is suitable for preparing in advance and easy to freeze.

🛒 **Ingredients:**

- ✔ 30 g round (short) grain rice
- ✔ ½ small spring onion
- ✔ 1 tsp butter or olive oil
- ✔ 3 spears of green asparagus
- ✔ 50 g chicken breast fillet

✏ **Notes:**

👍 **Finger food:**

1. Wash the spring onion and cut into thin rings.

2. Briefly sauté the rice with the spring onions in butter or olive oil in a pan, cover with water and simmer over a medium heat, stirring constantly. Keep adding water and stirring until the rice is cooked through.

3. Wash and peel the asparagus and cut into 1 cm pieces.

4. Rinse the chicken, pat dry, cut into finger-sized pieces and cook with the asparagus in a steamer for 10 minutes.

5. Stir the asparagus and chicken into the rice.

6. Allow the meal to cool to a safe eating temperature and offer it to your baby.

🥣 **Puree:**

1. Wash the spring onion and cut into thin rings.

2. Briefly sauté the rice with the spring onions in butter or olive oil in a pan, then cover with water and simmer over a medium heat, stirring constantly. Keep adding water and stirring until the rice is cooked through.

3. Wash and peel the asparagus and cut into 1 cm pieces.

4. Rinse the chicken, pat dry, cut into small pieces and steam with the asparagus in a steamer for 10 minutes.

5. Add the asparagus and chicken to the rice and blend with a hand blender until smooth.

6. Allow the puree to cool to a safe eating temperature and offer a few spoons thereof to your baby.

Sweet potato pancakes with hummus

🕐 **Minutes: 30** | 👤 **ready for solids** | 🍴 **Portions: 1-2**

♥ **Info:**

As simple as this dish sounds, it has all the important ingredients for a balanced meal. It contains iron as a nutrient thanks to the chickpeas and eggs. Refined with a little lemon, it not only expands the range of flavors that your baby will get to know, but the vitamin C from it also helps to optimally utilize the iron.

🛒 **Ingredients:**

- ✔ ½ small sweet potato
- ✔ 1 tbsp spelt flour (finger food recipe only)
- ✔ 1 organic egg (finger food recipe only)
- ✔ 50 g chickpeas (tin or jar)
- ✔ 1 tbsp fresh lemon juice
- ✔ ½ tsp oregano

👍 **Finger food:**

1. Peel the sweet potato, cut into small pieces and cook in a steamer for 10 minutes. Then mash the sweet potato pieces in a bowl with a fork and leave to cool slightly.

2. Beat the egg and mix this along with the spelt flour and sweet potato mash to form a batter.

3. Fry the tablespoon-sized pancakes in a pan with a little oil for 1 minute on each side and leave to cool to eating temperature.

4. Blend the chickpeas with a little water from the tin, the fresh lemon juice and the oregano in a bowl using a hand blender.

5. Spread the hummus on the pancakes and offer them to your baby.

🥣 **Puree:**

1. Peel the sweet potato, cut into small pieces and cook in a steamer for 10 minutes.

2. Blend the sweet potato pieces, chickpeas with a little water from the tin, the fresh lemon juice and the oregano in a bowl with a hand blender.

3. Allow to cool to a safe eating temperature and offer your baby a few spoons full.

💡 **Tip:**

✔ The hummus is suitable as a dip for vegetable sticks and pasta.

Tomatoes, beans and beef

🕐 **Minutes: 20**   👤 **ready for solids**   🍴 **Portions: 1-2**

❤️ **Info:**

This recipe is one of my family's favorites.

🛒 **Ingredients:**

- ✔ ½ spring onion
- ✔ 100 g organic minced beef
- ✔ 50 g kidney beans (tin or jar)
- ✔ 1 tomato
- ✔ ½ bell pepper
- ✔ ½ tsp thyme

✏️ **Notes:**

👍 **Finger food:**

1. Wash the spring onion, cut into small pieces and fry in a non-stick pan with the minced beef.

2. Wash the tomato and bell pepper, cut into small pieces and add to the pan.

3. Add the kidney beans to the pan with a little water from the tin or jar and the thyme and simmer for 10 minutes.

4. Allow the meal to cool to a safe eating temperature and offer it to your baby.

🥣 **Puree:**

1. Wash the spring onion, cut into small pieces and fry in a non-stick pan with the minced beef.

2. Wash the tomato and bell pepper, cut into small pieces and add to the pan.

3. Add the kidney beans to the pan with a little water from the tin and the thyme and simmer for 10 minutes.

4. Then blend mixture to a puree with a hand blender.

5. Allow the puree to cool to a safe eating temperature and offer to your baby.

💡 **Tip:**

- This dish is easy to prepare and freeze. You can then reheat it in the microwave or in saucepan.

Mealtime trials

Common challenges when introducing solids

There are challenges in the period of introducing complementary food. Let's look at the most common ones and how to handle them in the most baby-friendly way.

Your baby shows no interest in solids despite being ready

When your baby reaches six months and shows the three physiological signs of readiness for complementary foods, they are theoretically ready to start eating. However, it's common for babies to prefer their usual breast milk or formula over new foods.

Don't stress too much. Your baby doesn't need to immediately eat a lot of complementary foods just because they are ready. Even if other babies seem to be eating more, that's okay.

It's recommended that by eight months, your baby should start eating small amounts of complementary foods. There's still plenty of time for your baby to adapt.

My tips:
1. Eat together and model eating behavior.
2. Offer more than just purees.
3. Establish a routine.
4. Allow your baby to eat independently.

Your baby doesn't want to be spoon-fed

Babies naturally crave independence. It's common for them to reject the spoon. And honestly, who likes to be fed?

The simplest solution is to let your baby eat independently. If your baby is ready for complementary foods, they can bring the spoon to their mouth by themselves. You can help by filling the spoon with puree and placing it in front of them.

Extra tips:
- Use 2 to 3 spoons so you can quickly provide more food.
- Offer baby-friendly finger foods for self-feeding.

Your baby doesn't like purees at all

Whether store-bought or homemade, your baby refuses every puree? This is not uncommon. Some babies simply don't like the texture and prefer to eat "real" food.

In this case, I recommend exploring baby-led weaning (BLW) approach to complementary feeding. It could be the solution for your baby!

Your baby loves only pureed food

Some babies love purees and continue to prefer them even at 10, 11, 12 months or older.

Tips:
1. Gradually increase the texture of the puree to help your baby get used to it.
2. Offer snacks that your baby can hold, like corn cakes, mango pits, chicken drumsticks, corn on the cob, or bread crusts to gnaw on. This helps your baby's sensitive mouth develop.
3. Keep offering firmer foods even if your baby gags. Gagging is part of the learning process and improves with practice.

Your baby makes funny faces while eating and spits everything out

Two different things are happening here, which parents often misunderstand.

1.	The inside of your baby's mouth is extremely sensitive and has only experienced the sweet taste of breast milk or formula. When new foods cause a burst of flavors, it stimulates all the nerves and senses in your baby's face. This often leads to funny faces and even shuddering, much like when we bite into a lemon.

2.	This is completely normal and doesn't mean your baby dislikes the food. It's simply new and they need to get used to it. Spitting out food doesn't mean your baby dislikes it either. It's a protective mechanism against choking. Anything that isn't ready to be swallowed gets pushed out. This is great because it means your baby is protecting itself very effectively.

Your baby gags and vomits when eating solids

I know, this scenario is really distressing to observe and can quickly cause panic for parents. But gagging is a natural protective mechanism to prevent choking and suffocation. Your baby has this wonderful ability and usually doesn't need help. I know, it's hard to watch.

This is happening in baby's mouth:
A piece of food gets too far back in the mouth before it's ready to be swallowed, triggering the gag reflex to push it out. The strength of the gag reflex can vary greatly, and it's common for babies to vomit as well. Even so, you can trust your baby, and with practice, this will improve quickly!

Let's clarify:
- Gagging and choking are not the same.
- As long es your baby is loud and active it doesn't need help – that's gagging.
- If it is still, turns blue, and no longer makes any noise it needs your help – that's choking!

I strongly recommend completing a baby first aid course to be sure to know what to do in case of serious choking.

Your baby stuffs their mouth too full

Overstuffing and shoveling food into their mouth is a phase most babies go through, and there's a good reason for it! Your baby is learning all about the inside of their mouth.

They fill their mouth to learn what "too much" is. Then, they learn how to spit out excess food, take bites of the right size, and differentiate between textures without having to see the food. The amazing natural protection mechanism, gagging, keeps them safe from choking during this process.

So, it's completely normal for your baby to shovel food into their mouth. I understand it can be hard to watch sometimes. Serve small portions of complementary foods on the plate and add more as needed.

Your baby doesn't want to touch the food

Here's what you can do if your baby doesn't want to touch their food:
1. Get your baby's attention at the table and minimize distractions.
2. Be a role model and demonstrate how to eat. Eating together can work wonders.
3. Describe to your baby what's on the menu and what's on the plate. Rather describe color, texture and taste than only saying "it's yummy."
4. Offer larger pieces of food, like a whole banana, half an avocado, or a mango pip with lots of flesh around it.

Your baby has constipation

The most common reasons for constipation in babies are:
- Starting complementary foods too early, for example, at 4 months, before the baby is ready.
- Feeding too much complementary food.
- Replacing breast/formula milk too early, which means offering too little of it.
- Offering constipating foods.

This may help for your baby's constipation:

- Feed less complementary food and allow self-feeding.
- Offer more breast/formula milk.
- Provide stool-softening foods like natural yogurt.
- Offer baby-friendly fruits like kiwi.
- Include baby-friendly, fiber-rich foods.

What's next?

The next steps in introducing complementary foods

You've probably had an experience-rich first month of complementary feeding. You will now find it easy to recognize when and how your baby wants to eat. It may even have already discovered its favorite foods. The introduction of complementary foods is not over yet, but you should now have gained confidence in how you can help your baby become a healthy and happy eater.

A lot will happen in your baby's development over the next few months and this will also affect the introduction of complementary foods. Developmental leaps, appearing teeth, possible illnesses and other circumstances can often have a negative impact on the introduction of complementary foods and eating behavior. It is not uncommon for babies to completely refuse to eat for days and prefer to drink their usual milk. Don't let this put you off. Give your baby what it needs and stick to the routine. After a few days, it's usually over again.

In the following section, I have compiled information that is important for the further complementary feeding period. This way you can continue to feel confident about offering your baby food. You will learn how to create a balanced baby plate and when you can introduce more meals. The pincer grasp is another milestone in your baby's development and you will learn what changes it brings to complementary feeding.

I have also put together some interesting facts about cow's milk, dairy products, eggs, nuts and sugar in complementary foods. You will also receive a list of over 100 foods that you can offer in the first year of life so that you can provide as varied a selection as possible.

A balanced baby plate

Putting together a balanced baby plate is not as complicated as it sounds. Ideally, only three types of food are needed. If a meal doesn't consist of all three types every time, that's not a problem. In the following, I will show you a recommendation to give you an idea of how you can create a balanced baby plate.

What should be on a balanced baby plate?

- ✔ Vegetables or fruit: They provide lots of vitamins and additional fluids, which aids digestion.

- ✔ Sources of iron: Iron is important for brain development, for example. Good sources of iron are meat, fish and eggs, but also oats, lentils and chickpeas in combination with vitamin C.

- ✔ High-calorie foods: These provide sufficient energy, of which the little ones need a lot. These include, for example, bread, pasta, grain, oils, nut butter and avocado.[53]

The previous recipes, starting from the 3rd week onwards and the recipes from my complementary food cookbooks generally follow this basic scheme and contain these three main ingredients that belong on a balanced baby plate. Using two example dishes, I would like to show you how you can easily apply this rule.

Example 1: Baby muesli made from oats, nut butter and fruit

- ✔ Oats and nut butter are both high in calories and iron.

- ✔ The fruit provides the vitamins, including those needed to utilize the bound iron in oats and nuts.

Example 2: Whole-wheat pasta with Bolognese

- ✔ Pasta is the high-calorie food.

- ✔ The tomatoes in the sauce are the vegetables.

- ✔ The meat in the sauce is the source of iron.

In its ten rules for a healthy diet, the German Nutrition Society recommends eating meat two to three times a week and fish once or twice a week.[54] This rule can provide you with further guidance when it comes to offering your baby balanced complementary foods. It not only applies to complementary foods, but can also be applied to the entire family's diet. You can find many more examples of how to put together a balanced complementary food plate on my Instagram account and on my website.

How many meals should your baby have a day?

In the first part of the book (page 42), I already talked about the quantity of baby meals. Now it's about the frequency of daily meals. This is (as always) a very individual matter, depending on your child and your daily routine. The aim is to have three main meals and two snacks a day at around twelve months. In addition, breast/formula milk should continue to be given as required. The following gives a direction to follow, but in the end your baby decides how much solid food and milk it likes.

From eight months

In the first month, you probably offered one or two meals a day. This can be continued without hesitation until the eighth month if it suits you and your baby. The breast/formula milk will continue to provide nutrients.

From eight months on, you can already offer three main meals. Ideally breakfast, lunch and dinner. If your baby is already eating large quantities, this is of course a great development. But if not, this is completely normal at this age and absolutely nothing to worry about. It's still just about learning the eating routine and eating in general. Your baby should continue to breastfeed on demand or be offered infant formula as usual. Ideally, this should happen 30 to 60 minutes before and after each meal. This way, your baby can continue to drink its fill.

According to the many messages I receive about this, it seems that there is an increased refusal to eat in this age. Up to this point, the baby has been eating "well", but suddenly all complementary foods are rejected. This is not unusual. At this age in particular, a lot is happening during development, which can affect the introduction of complementary foods. As a rule, this is a temporary phase.

My recommendation: Continue to offer complementary foods as usual, but especially breast/formula milk. This is because there is often an increased demand for it during such phases. This way you can ensure a sufficient supply of nutrients.

From eleven months

At around eleven months, the intake of nutrients from sources other than breast milk/formula becomes more important. You can therefore introduce a morning and afternoon snack from this point onwards. You may already notice that your baby is asking for less milk or is drinking less milk in total. This is a sign that he is already able to eat his fill. If this is not yet the case, stay relaxed and stick to your routine. Give your baby the time it needs.

Five meals a day is a guideline. For a long time, we only managed four meals a day until Ida was two years old, as our daily routine didn't allow for anything else - and that was perfectly fine. So, follow your gut feeling and the needs of your child. You need to find out what works for your baby best.

The pincer grasp

You will probably notice another milestone in your baby's motor development around the ninth month. Your baby's fine motor skills will improve. They are increasingly able to pick up small things with their thumb and index finger - this is known as the pincer grasp.[55]

As soon as your baby has mastered this grip to some extent, you can start cutting finger food into small cubes. This also encourages motor development and brings some variety to the plate. From then on, you no longer have to offer the vegetables in finger food sticks, but can cut them into two-by-two cm pieces, for example, as your baby can also pick up smaller things and put them in their mouth.

Practicing the pincer grasp can also be perfectly integrated during playtime by repeatedly offering small things to pick up and move. Create opportunities for your baby to squeeze and pull things and encourage pointing. Holding cutlery will also become easier for your baby from now on. That's why you should also let them practice at every meal.

When your baby is older and has mastered the pincer grasp, I recommend going back to larger food shapes. This will prevent your child from still wanting to have their bread cut into bite-sized pieces later on and encourage to take bites to practice this skill even more.

Dairy milk, dairy products and alternatives

Dairy milk and dairy products for babies is a much-discussed topic. Whether you want to give your child cow's milk and products made from this is up to you. There are just a few things you should bear in mind. That's why I'd like to debunk some myths below, give you a general recommendation and go into more facts. But first things first:

- ✔ Dairy milk is **never** a substitute for breast/formula milk!

For a long time, it was recommended that dairy milk and products made from it should be avoided in the first year of life. This recommendation was upheld for two reasons:

- ✔ On the one hand, it was thought that dairy should be introduced later because it is an allergen. Today, the opposite is recommended, as I have already explained in the chapter on food allergies (page 54).

- ✔ On the other hand, it was to be avoided because it contains too much protein and therefore puts a strain on the baby's kidneys. However, today there are also guidelines for the safe amount of dairy and dairy products for babies.

How much dairy milk can my baby drink?

Dairy milk is not suitable as a beverage in the first year of life; only breast/formula milk or small amounts of water should therefore be offered to drink. Otherwise, there is the danger that dairy could be seen as a substitute for infant milk. However, up to 200 ml of dairy milk per day is permitted in processed form, for example in a puree or in other foods.[56] From the first birthday, the amount increases to 300 ml daily.[57]

How many dairy milk products can my baby eat?

In the first year of life, babies are allowed to consume a total of 200 g of processed dairy per day. Here are a few examples of what your baby could eat per day:

- ✔ 200 g milk porridge or
- ✔ 120 g natural yogurt or
- ✔ 20 g butter or
- ✔ 30 g low-salt, mild cheese or
- ✔ a combination of the above products

Very small amounts of cream cheese, cottage cheese or cream (sauces) are also possible. When introducing complementary foods without puree, for example, around 100 g of natural yoghurt, 5 g of butter and 20 g of cheese per day would be one way of reaching the recommended amount of dairy.

From around the first year of life, the amounts of dairy products per day can be slowly increased to 300 g. The quantities do not include infant formula. Although infant formula is also made from dairy, it is so heavily modified that it is not included here.

Whether you want to give your baby dairy products is your decision. Fact is that we don't need dairy to survive and we can also get the nutrients we need from other foods.[58]

Are dairy alternatives allowed?

Due to the great demand for plant-based alternatives to cow's milk, more and more plant-based milk products are becoming available. Oat, soy, or rice milk are well-known alternatives to dairy. Again, these are neither a substitute for breast/formula milk nor suitable to drink for babies under one year old. You can use plant milks as a substitute for dairy in processed foods.

Plant-based milk substitutes are also suitable in moderation. However, when choosing the right product, it is important to check the list of ingredients. Many vegan products contain additives such as sugar, salt, flavorings, preservatives, and stabilizers, all which are not necessarily recommended for a baby.

I have mainly used oat milk for my daughters since they started complementary feeding. The brand "Oatly" offers an oat milk that only contains four ingredients. Water, oats, rapeseed oil, and a reasonable amount of salt. There is also a version with added calcium. Alternatively, I also make my own oat milk without salt. You can find the recipe on my website.

Eggs in the first year of life

Eggs are also particularly important in complementary foods. Like cow's milk, eggs are an allergen and contain a lot of protein, which can put a strain on immature baby kidneys.

The recommendation that eggs are not allowed in the first year of life is no longer up to date. Even though eggs are an allergen, babies are allowed to eat them when they are ready to be start on solids.[59] The only thing to watch out for is the right amount and correct preparation. Eggs contain important nutrients, including iron, which is so important for development. This is why eggs also play an important role in the introduction of vegetarian complementary foods.

One or two eggs a week are safe. You can offer eggs as a complementary food in the form of boiled eggs or processed in waffles, cakes, muffins and cookies.[60] The eggs should always be fully cooked so that there is no risk of salmonella poisoning.

I recommend that you offer your baby eggs (including processed eggs) regularly, but in moderation. If you can, choose organic eggs over conventional eggs, as the hens' feed is more controlled and the hens live in a better environment.

Nuts for babies

When we think of nuts and babies, the first things that come to mind are allergies and the risk of choking. However, nuts are suitable for babies when they are ready for solids, as long as they are offered in a baby-friendly way. There is no medical reason - such as allergy prevention[61] - not to give babies nuts to eat.

Whole or coarsely chopped nuts are not suitable for babies or small children. Nuts in this form should be offered from the age of five at the earliest. The reason for this is the risk of chocking or inhalation.

Processed nut flour or raw nut butter, on the other hand, are valuable sources of nutrients and are among the foods rich in iron and calories. I recommend that you particular include nut butters in your baby's diet.

For example, you can always stir a teaspoon of nut butter into your breakfast cereal or use it as an additional ingredient when baking waffles, muffins or pancakes. I also like to specifically use nut butter in my baby food baking recipes. And as a snack, I sometimes just use a teaspoon of almond butter. It is high in calories, contains iron and other nutrients, and is filling.

Sugar during the complementary feeding period

Not all sugars are the same. The form in which we consume sugar is crucial for a healthy diet. Many unprocessed foods contain sugar and this is not necessarily a bad thing. Isolated white processed sugar is utilized differently by our body than fructose, for example, which is contained in an apple. It also makes a difference to digestion whether the sugar is drunk or chewed.

Industrially produced sugar, which is mainly found in processed foods, can have negative effects if consumed in excess. This can result in an increased risk of obesity and tooth decay. In the first year of life during the introduction of complementary foods, it is worth avoiding this sugar in order to minimize the above-mentioned risks.

As already mentioned, honey and maple syrup are not safe foods for babies, at least until their first birthday. Sugar substitutes such as sweeteners, erythritol, xylitol, stevia and other flavor powders are also not suitable for babies.

Sweetening with fruit and vegetables

There are plenty of ways to enjoy sweet treats with a little creativity in preparation. If you would like to explore these options, you can take a look at my book "Sugar-free baking for babies (Christmas Edition)" (page 189). Fruit and vegetables are healthy, even though they may contain fructose, because they contain lots of vitamins, minerals, fiber and other valuable nutrients. Vegetables are generally less sweet than fruit, but there are also vegetables such as pumpkins or sweet potatoes that have a good measure of sweetness to them.

Eating fruit and vegetables in their original form, i.e. not as "squeezies/pouches" or juice, is ideal for optimal digestion. This is because the digestive process begins with chewing.

Solid foods list

Vegetables and fruits

- Apple
- Apricot
- Asparagus
- Avocado
- Banana
- Beet
- Bell pepper
- Blackberry
- Blueberry
- Broccoli
- Brussels sprouts
- Carrot
- Cauliflower
- Celeriac
- Celery stalks
- Cherry
- Clementine
- Corn
- Cucumber
- Damson plum
- Date
- Dragon fruit
- Eggplant
- Fennel
- Fig
- Grape
- Grapefruit
- Green beans
- Honeydew melon
- Kiwi
- Kohlrabi
- Leek
- Lemon
- Lime
- Lychee
- Mango
- Mirabelle plum
- Nectarine
- Onion
- Orange
- Papaya
- Parsnip
- Passion fruit
- Peach
- Pear
- Peas
- Physalis
- Pineapple
- Plantain
- Plum
- Pomegranate
- Potato
- Pumpkin
- Quince
- Radish
- Raisins
- Raspberry
- Rhubarb
- Spinach
- Spring onion
- Squash
- Strawberry
- Swede
- Sweet potato
- Tangerine
- Tomato
- Turnip
- Watermelon
- Yam
- Zucchini

High-calorie foods

- Avocado
- Almond butter
- Bagel
- Bread roll
- Bulgur
- Butter
- Cake
- Cashew butter
- Cheese
- Chia seeds
- Coconut flakes
- Cookies
- Corn
- Couscous
- Cream cheese
- Date
- French toast
- Ground hemp seeds
- Hazelnut butter
- Muffins
- Noodles
- Oat flakes
- Oils
- Pancakes
- Peanut butter
- Pita bread
- Pizza
- Pretzels
- Quinoa
- Rice
- Semolina
- Spelt
- Sponge cake
- Waffles
- Whole wheat bread
- Yogurt

Iron-rich foods

- Beef
- Black beans
- Chia seeds
- Chicken
- Chickpea noodles
- Chickpeas
- Cod
- Eggs
- Flaxseed
- Green beans
- Hemp seeds
- Hummus
- Kidney beans
- Lamb
- Lentil
- Lentil noodles
- Linseed
- Minced meat
- Pancakes
- Pork
- Salmon (wild caught)
- Turkey
- White beans

Baby-friendly herbs

- ✔ Aniseed
- ✔ Basil
- ✔ Bay leaf (laurel)
- ✔ Caraway seeds
- ✔ Carnation
- ✔ Coriander
- ✔ Cress
- ✔ Dill
- ✔ Garlic
- ✔ Ginger
- ✔ Lemon balm
- ✔ Mild pepper
- ✔ Mint
- ✔ Oregano
- ✔ Parsley
- ✔ Rosemary
- ✔ Sage
- ✔ Tarragon
- ✔ Thyme
- ✔ Turmeric
- ✔ Wild garlic

Frequently asked questions

FAQ on complementary foods

I always receive a lot of questions from parents about complementary feeding. Some of them occur often. That's why I've bundled the most frequently asked questions about complementary feeding that I haven't answered in this book together in this chapter.

My baby was born prematurely - when is it ready for complementary food?

The baby is expected to be ready for complementary feeding at the amended age. Here is an example: Your baby was born four weeks too early. Normal complementary feeding maturity begins around the sixth month of life, so your baby would be expected to be ready for complementary feeding around the seventh month of life.

Do I always have to buy organic food for my baby?

There are some foods that should be bought of organic quality, as they are demonstrably less contaminated with harmful substances. These include, for example, foods that grow in the ground, such as potatoes and carrots, but also berries. In general, of course, it is a question of financial means. If you can't afford organic products on a regular basis, you should still opt for normal fruit and vegetables rather than eliminating them from your diet due to the lack of organic quality. In this case, regional products may be an alternative for you.

When does solid food replace the milk meal?

Not at first, as breast/formula milk should be offered on demand until your baby independently decides to refuse the milk meal. Remember that it is still important to at least offer the milk meal, especially during an illness or a phase of food refusal.

When can I put my baby in the highchair to eat?

Occupational therapists recommend that babies should not be placed in a highchair until they are able to move to a sitting position independently, either from crawling or standing. This usually happens around the ninth month. Until then, the recommendation is to offer your baby solid food while sitting in your lap.

Does my baby need snacks between meals?

From the age of eleven months, you can offer one snack in the morning and one in the afternoon. I wouldn't offer any more snacks, otherwise your baby may not be hungry at the main meals.

My baby eats almost nothing at 8, 9, 10, 11 or 12 months. What can I do?

In principle, it is not unusual for some babies to eat only minimal amounts at this age. However, if you feel that your baby should be eating more, review your routine and the times of milk and complementary meals. Babies often don't eat much at this age if they are either too full or too hungry. Other circumstances such as illness, teething, or a developmental leap can also be responsible for this. Don't let this put you off. As a rule, these are phases and some babies only discover eating for themselves after their first birthday. Every baby has its own pace. However, if your baby does not seem healthy you should talk to your pediatrician. An iron deficiency can cause loss of appetite. Another possibility is a tongue tie, which can make it hard to eat for your baby.

My baby pulls a face when he tries something. Doesn't he like my food?

When a baby tastes something for the first time, all the taste buds in the mouth and the muscles are activated, causing the face to contort. For us adults, this gives the impression that the baby doesn't like it. But this is not the case. It usually only becomes clear whether a baby really doesn't like a certain food after trying it several times. So don't give up and offer it again.

My baby always bites off big chunks and stuffs their mouth full. I'm afraid that it will choke.

As nerve-wracking as it is, part of learning to eat is finding out how much fits into the mouth and how big a bite needs to be in order to be able to chew and swallow afterwards. Moreover, it is usually not the large pieces that pose a choking risk and what cannot be swallowed is usually spat out again.

Do I have to add oil to the complementary food?

You can, but do not have to, add oil to complementary foods, whether puree or finger food. The background to this recommendation is that some nutrients and vitamins require oil for optimal utilization in the body. However, as the usual breast/formula milk is still available during the introduction of solid foods and this contains all the necessary fats, the addition of oil is not necessary but could add some extra calories to the meal.

I have been advised not to offer my baby breast/formula milk so that more solid food is eaten. Should I do this?

No! Depriving your baby of the needed milk, for whatever reason, is never acceptable. Please refrain from such advice, no matter who it comes from, and give your baby the milk it wants.

At twelve months, my baby is still drinking a lot of milk. What can I do?

I can only emphasize again and again: No baby works according to a textbook. But babies have very well-functioning instincts and skills. If your baby wants to drink breast/formula milk, then give it in any case. Nevertheless, continue to offer complementary foods regularly. When your baby is ready, it will eat more. Again, it's important that you don't compare your baby with others as the stress and doubts that arise are often only there because of comparisons. As long as your baby seems healthy and happy, you don't have to do anything except respond to their needs. If your baby does not seem healthy you should talk to your pediatrician.

My baby doesn't want to eat with cutlery. Do you have a recommendation?

I generally recommend offering baby its own cutlery with every meal right from the start of complementary feeding. This gives your baby the opportunity to copy you eating with cutlery. Babies often quickly figure out how this works. Of course, it may be that your baby simply prefers to eat with their hands because it is so much more interesting from a sensory point of view. I wouldn't stop this kind of discovery. Over time, all children learn or decide to use cutlery.

My baby keeps throwing the food onto the floor. What can I do?

At the very beginning of complementary feeding, it is simply a game for babies. They try out what happens when food lands on the floor. Does it make a noise? Does it move around on the floor or does it stay there? This is part of the discovery process. Over time, throwing food down or wiping it off the table can be a sign that your baby is full and finished eating. Here you can teach baby to set the plate aside instead.

I am unsure about offering certain foods (nuts/ fish/ meat/ spices). Isn't my baby too young for this?

As long as the foods are prepared in a baby-friendly way and are not on the list of unsuitable foods, your baby can and may eat all foods from the complementary food stage. If you are very unsure about allergies, talk to your pediatrician.

Everyone is advising me to start with puree. Do I have to?

Quite emphatically: no! The introduction of solid food in the form of puree is widespread, but not necessarily the only way. Babies are able to eat foods with more texture once they are ready for complementary foods. The baby-led weaning approach particularly demonstrates this. Follow your gut instinct and try out what works best for you and your baby. There is nothing wrong with a combination of puree and finger food.

I am very scared that my child will choke. What can I do?

You are not alone in this fear. I would even say that many parents are most afraid of their baby choking on food. What helps is education and the necessary background knowledge. I have summarized the most important information on this topic in the chapter "Gagging and choking" (page 47).

My baby sleeps very badly, should I give him more to eat?

A persistent complementary feeding myth that is still around. The introduction of solid foods and baby's sleep are not directly related. Longer sleep is a developmental process. Very few babies wake up because they are hungry, but rather because the sleep cycle is over and they have problems transitioning to the next one on their own. A very full tummy can mean the exact opposite.

Franka's blog:

www.babyidaisst.com

About the book

The approach

This basic book for baby-friendly nutrition is a modern guide for parents who want to start complementary feeding and need a safe starting aid. It deals with starting complementary feeding with finger foods and purees, according to the latest findings, moving away from strictly scheduled puree towards modern, needs-oriented food learning. The information has been carefully researched and the recipes thoroughly tested by the author.

This book does not contain a typical baby puree recipes with carrots and mashed potatoes, full of glossy photos and incomprehensible theory - it is a guide that can't be found elsewhere, because it combines baby food and puree and is understandable for everyone. The layout of the book has been kept deliberately minimalist; unnecessary explanations and digressions have been avoided. Instead, the focus is on the chapters and recipes with clear instructions, because that's all you need for a safe, baby-friendly solid food introduction.

But, that's not all: This book was produced fairly and to a high standard by our small veggie + publishing house. We work with regional designers and editors and have many of our books produced entirely in Germany. We treat all partners involved in the production chain fairly - and pay them accordingly. All of them are small and medium-sized companies who put their heart and soul into their work and with whom we pursue a common goal: to produce high-quality products that make our readers happy.

Our books are produced under sustainable conditions, protect the environment and promote the regional economy. And that is exactly what you are supporting when you buy this book.

High five for that!

Sources and literature

1   Renz-Polster: Understanding children. From Zoff ums Beifüttern,
     https://www.kinder-verstehen.de/mein-werk/blog/zoff-ums-beifuettern/, 2016,
     accessed on 8.3.2023.

2   Bührer: Ernährung gesunder Säuglinge, in: Monatsschreiben Kinderheilkunde
     (DGKJ), 2014, p. 532.

3   Zimmer: So isst die Welt, in: GEOlino, https://www.geo.de/geolino/kreativ/
     9146-rtkl-so-isst-die-welt, 2005, accessed on March 8, 2023.

4   Fangupo, Heath, Williams et. al: A Baby-Led Approach to Eating Solids and
     Risk of Choking, in: Pediatrics, 2016, vol. 138, no. 4, p. 6.

5   Unicef United Kingdom: Introducing solid foods. Giving your baby a better
     start in life, https://www.unicef.org.uk/babyfriendly/wp-content/uploads/
     sites/2/2008/02/Start4Life-Introducing-Solid-Foods-2015.pdf, 2015, accessed
     8.3.2023.

6   Rapley, Murkett: Baby-led weaning: Das Grundlagenbuch, Kösel-Verlag, 2nd
     edition 2021, p. 37 ff.

7   Davis: Self-selection of diet by newly weaned infants: an experimental study,
     in: American Journal of Diseases in Childhood, 1928, Vol. 36, No. 4, pp. 651ff.

8   Dewey: Guiding principles for complementary feeding of the breastfed child,
     in: Pan American Health Organization, 2003, p. 10 f.

9   Largo: Babyjahre Entwicklung und Erziehung in den ersten vier Jahren. Piper
     Verlag, 8th edition 2007, p. 187 ff.

10   Nicklaus: The role of food experiences during early childhood in food pleasure
     learning, in: Appetite, 2016, vol. 104, pp. 3-9.

11   Imlau: Mein kompetentes Baby, Kösel-Verlag, 5th edition 2016, p. 78 ff.

12   Renz-Polster: Kinder verstehen. Von Zoff ums Beifüttern,
     https://www.kinder-verstehen.de/mein-werk/blog/zoff-ums-beifuettern/,
     2016, accessed on 8.3.2023.

13   Imlau: Mein kompetentes Baby, Kösel-Verlag, 5th edition 2016, p. 96 f.

14   Bührer: Ernährung gesunder Säuglinge, in: Monatsschreiben Kinderheilkunde
     (DGKJ), 2014, p. 532.

15   Medela Medizintechnik: Stillen über den sechsten Monat hinaus: Was sind die
     Vorteile?, https://www.medela.de/stillen/deine-stillzeit/stillen-nach-dem-
     sechsten-monat#reference, 2022, accessed 1.1.2023.

16   Nicklaus: The role of food experiences during early childhood in food pleasure learning, in: Appetite, 2016, vol. 104, pp. 3-9.

17   Eugster: Babyernährung gesund & richtig: B(r)eikost und Fingerfood nach dem 6. Lebensmonat, Urban & Fischer Verlag/Elsevier GmbH, 3rd edition 2013, p. 10.

18   Sgarz: Welche Rolle spielt der Darm bei Allergien?, https://www.allergosan.com/de/blog/welche-rolle-spielt-der-darm-bei-allergien/, 2022, accessed 1.1.2023.

19   Bührer: Ernährung gesunder Säuglinge, in: Monatsschreiben Kinderheilkunde (DGKJ), 2014, Vol. 162, No. 6, p. 532.

20   Unicef United Kingdom: Introducing solid foods. Giving your baby a better start in life, https://www.unicef.org.uk/babyfriendly/wp-content/uploads/sites/2/2008/02/Start4Life-Introducing-Solid-Foods-2015.pdf, 2015, accessed on 8.3.2023.

21   WHO: International Code of Marketing of Breast-milk Substitutes: Annex to WHA Resolution 34.22, https://www.stillen-institut.com/media/kodex-1981de.pdf, 1981, accessed 3/8/2023.

22   Unicef United Kingdom: Introducing solid foods. Giving your baby a better start in life, https://www.unicef.org.uk/babyfriendly/wp-content/uploads/sites/2/2008/02/Start4Life-Introducing-Solid-Foods-2015.pdf, 2015, accessed on 8.3.2023.

23   Rapley, Murkett: Baby-led weaning: Das Grundlagenbuch, Kösel-Verlag, 2nd edition 2021, p., p 66f.

24   Schmid: Mamaclever. 7 Lebensmittel für Babys, die zu leicht und zu dünn sind,, https://www.mamaclever.de/2020/04/08/7-kalorienreiche-lebensmittel-fuer-duenne-babys/, 2020, accessed on 8.3.2023.

25   Morison, Taylor, Haszard et al: How different are baby-led weaning and conventional complementary feeding? A cross-sectional study of infants aged 6-8 months, in: BMJ Open, 2016, p. 1 ff.

26   Davis: Self-selection of diet by newly weaned infants: an experimental study, in: American Journal of Diseases in Childhood, 1928, Vol. 36, No. 4, pp. 651ff.

27   Rapley, Murkett: Baby-led weaning: Das Grundlagenbuch, Kösel-Verlag, 2nd edition 2021, p 11, 73.

28   WHO: Infant and young child feeding, https://www.who.int/en/news-room/fact-sheets/detail/infant-and-young-child-feeding, 2021, accessed on 8.3.2023.

29   Dittmar: Das gewünschteste Wunschkind. Leidern Stillkinder wirklich unter Esienmangel? Eine kritische Betrachtung der Studie, A critical examination of

the study, https://www.gewuenschtestes-wunschkind.de/2013/03/die-eisen-luge-warum-stillkinder-nicht.html, 2013, accessed on 8.3.2023.

30   Rapley, Murkett: Baby-led weaning: Das Grundlagenbuch, Kösel-Verlag, 2nd edition 2021, p 65f.

31   WHO: Infant and young child feeding, https://www.who.int/en/news-room/fact-sheets/detail/infant-and-young-child-feeding, 2021, accessed on 8.3.2023.

32   Rapley, Murkett: Baby-led weaning: Das Grundlagenbuch, Kösel-Verlag, 2nd edition 2021, p 36f.

33   Eugster: Babyernährung gesund & richtig: B(r)eikost und Fingerfood nach dem 6. Lebensmonat, Urban & Fischer Verlag/Elsevier GmbH, 3rd edition 2013, p. 7ff.

34   Davis: Self-selection of diet by newly weaned infants: an experimental study, in: American Journal of Diseases in Childhood, 1928, Vol. 36, No. 4, pp. 651ff.

35   Günther: Ernährung bei Eisenmangel, Springer-Verlag, 1st edition 2021, p. 43.

36   Stirling-Reed: How to wean your baby, Vermilion, 1st edition 2021, p. 66 ff.

37   Fangupo et. al: A Baby-Led Approach to Eating Solids and Risk of Choking, in: Pediatrics, 2016, vol. 138, no. 4, p. 2ff, https://www.researchgate.net/publication/308399495_A_Baby-Led_Approach_to_Eating_Solids_and_Risk_of_Choking, accessed on March 8, 2023.

38   Schäflein & Merz: Breifreibaby. Entspannt in die Beikost starten – mit breifreibaby, http://breifreibaby.de, 2018, accessed on 8.3.2023.

39   Stirling-Reed: How to wean your baby, Vermilion, 1st edition 2021, p. 45.

40   Stirling-Reed: How to wean your baby, Vermilion, 1st edition 2021, p. 45.

41   Fangupo et. al: A Baby-Led Approach to Eating Solids and Risk of Choking, in: Pediatrics, 2016, vol. 138, no. 4, p. 2ff, https://www.researchgate.net/publication/308399495_A_Baby-Led_Approach_to_Eating_Solids_and_Risk_of_Choking, retrieved on 8.3.2023.

42   Solid Starts. Water for Babies and Toddlers, https://solidstarts.com/water/, 2022, accessed 8.3.2023.

43   Solid Starts: Water for Babies and Toddlers, https://solidstarts.com/water/, 2022, accessed 8.3.2023.

44   Solid Starts: Water for Babies and Toddlers, https://solidstarts.com/water/, 2022, accessed 8.3.2023.

45 Kopp et al: S3-Leitlinie Allergieprävention, in: AWMF online. Das Portal der wissenschaftlichen Medizin, https://register.awmf.org/assets/guidelines/061-016l_S3_Allergiepraevention_2022-11.pdf, 2022, accessed on 8.3.2023.

46 Deutsches Grünes Kreuz e. V.: Muttermilch als Allergieschutz, in: Deutsches Grünes Kreuz e.V. Informationsportal für Gesundheit, https://dgk.de/gesundheit/allergie-haut/allergien/tipps-fuer-den-alltag/muttermilch-als-allergieschutz.html, 2002, accessed on 8.3.2023.

47 Sgarz: Welche Rolle spielt der Darm bei Allergien? https://www.allergosan.com/de/blog/welche-rolle-spielt-der-darm-bei-allergien/, 2022, accessed 1.1.2023.

48 Kopp et al: S3-Leitlinie Allergieprävention, in: AWMF online. Das Portal der wissenschaftlichen Medizin, https://register.awmf.org/assets/guidelines/061-016l_S3_Allergiepraevention_2022-11.pdf, 2022, accessed on 8.3.2023.

49 Institut für Produktqualität: Liste der in der EU kennzeichnungspflichtigen Allergene, https://www.produktqualitaet.com/de/lebensmittel/allergene/kennzeichnungspflichtige-allergene.html, 2011, retrieved on 8.3.2023.

50 Bundeszentrale für gesundheitliche Aufklärung: Kindergesundheit Info. Lebensmittelallergien bei Babys und Kleinkinder, https://www.kindergesundheit-info.de/themen/krankes-kind/erkrankungen/allergien/lebensmittelallergien/, 2022, accessed on 8.3.2023.

51 Netzwerk Gesund ins Leben: Ab wann brauchen Säuglinge zusätzlich Flüssigkeit?, https://www.gesund-ins-leben.de/fuer-fachkreise/bestens-unterstuetzt-durchs-1-lebensjahr/nachgefragt/ab-wann-brauchen-saeuglinge-zusaetzlich-fluessigkeit/, 2018, accessed 8.3.2023.

52 Solid Starts: Water for Babies and Toddlers, https://solidstarts.com/water/, 2022, accessed 8.3.2023.

53 Stirling-Reed: How to wean your baby, Vermilion, 1st edition 2021, p. 64.

54 Deutsche Gesellschaft für Ernährung e.V.: Vollwertig essen und trinken nach den 10 Regeln der DGE, https://www.dge.de/ernaehrungspraxis/vollwertige-ernaehrung/10-regeln-der-dge/, 2017, accessed on 8.3.2023.

55 Author unknown: Pinzettengriff in der Krippe, https://www.herder.de/kk/u3-glossar/pinzettengriff-u3/, retrieved on 8.3.2023.

56 Bundesanstalt für Landwirtschaft und Ernährung (BLE): Gesund ins Leben. Milch und Milchprodukte in der Beikostzeit, https://www.gesund-ins-leben.de/fuer-fachkreise/bestens-unterstuetzt-durchs-1-lebensjahr/

handlungsempfehlungen/beikost/milch-und-milchprodukte-in-der-beikostzeit/, 2017, accessed on 8.3.2023.

57   Verbraucherzentrale: Milch und Milchprodukte für Kinder: Das sollten Sie beachten, https://www.verbraucherzentrale.de/wissen/lebensmittel/gesund-ernaehren/milch-und-milchprodukte-fuer-kinder-das-sollten-sie-beachten-5988, 2022, accessed on 8.3.2023.

58   Tertilt: Milch: Macht sie uns krank, https://www.quarks.de/gesundheit/darum-ist-milch-nicht-giftig/, 2020, accessed on 8.3.2023.

59   Kopp et al: S3-Leitlinie Allergieprävention, in: AWMF online. Das Portal der wissenschaftlichen Medizin, https://register.awmf.org/assets/guidelines/061-016l_S3_Allergiepraevention_2022-11.pdf, 2022, accessed on 8.3.2023.

60   Christiansen: Hühnerei-Allergie Neue Tipps und Informationen, https://www.daab.de/blog/2023/01/huehnerei-allergie-neue-tipps-und-informationen/, 2023, accessed on 8.3.2023.

61   Kopp et al: S3-Leitlinie Allergieprävention, in: AWMF online. Das Portal der wissenschaftlichen Medizin, https://register.awmf.org/assets/guidelines/061-016l_S3_Allergiepraevention_2022-11.pdf, 2022, accessed on 8.3.2023.

About the author

Franka Lederbogen is the founder of the blog www.babyidaisst.com and the successful Instagram account @babyidaeats. She has been focusing on healthy eating for more than two decades and, since the birth of her two daughters, also on healthy baby food.

As an expert in introducing solids as complementary food, she combines her knowledge as a nutritionist, specialist in baby-friendly solid foods (whether in puree or not) and is the mom of two baby-led weaning babies. Through this guide, she shares how easy it can be to introduce complementary foods.

You now have the summary of all the theory she has learned and her personal experiences, thus showing a modern way of introducing baby-friendly complementary foods. The recipes she has developed are intended to help you as parent offer your baby a varied and healthy diet.

This is Franka

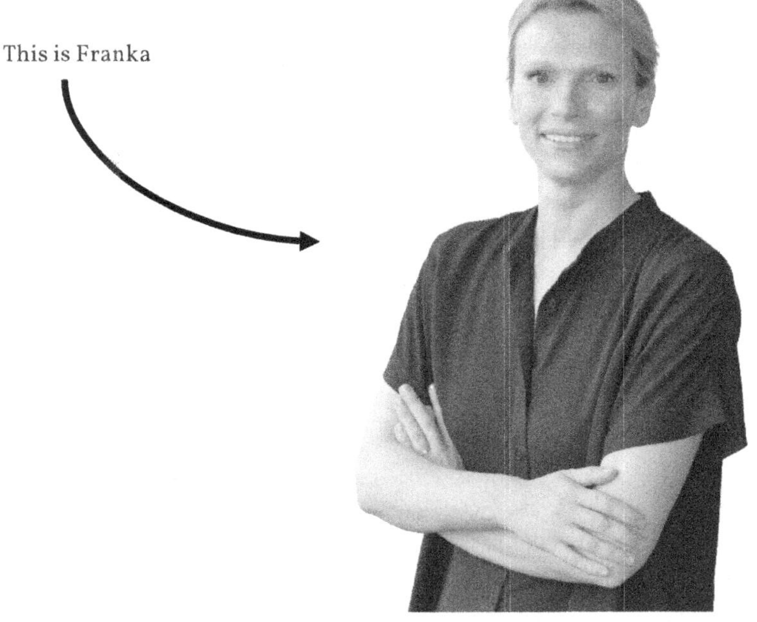

Thank you

Without the help of other people, I would not have been able to write and publish this book. I would therefore like to take this opportunity to thank you from the bottom of my heart.

Most of all, I would like to thank my readers and all the parents who have sought my help and put their trust in me so far. Thanks to your feedback and encouragement, I have decided to make this book even better. Thank you for your support.

A very big thank you goes to Tim Reichel, who made it possible for me to publish this project from the heart. Thank you for your professional input and your commitment to making this book a particularly good one.

I would also like to thank Hannah Dautzenberg for her valuable comments and expert support, which gave this book the necessary finishing touches. Further thanks go to Delia Hansen for her helpful proofreading and final corrections.

A big thank you also goes to my two daughters, who were so willing to test all my recipes. Finally, I would like to thank my husband, who always had motivating words for me in stressful times.

Thank you all very much.

Franka Lederbogen, December 2024

4-Ingredient BLW Recipes (6 Months Onwards)

The big baby-led weaning cookbook with simple recipes to start solids for babies from 6 months onwards

Order now: www.veggieplus.de/buecher

Sugar-free Baking for Babies
(Christmas Edition)

The big baking book with Christmas recipes

sugar-free, especially for babies and toddlers

📖 Order now: www.veggieplus.de/buecher

So isst dein Baby Beikost (Grundlagenbuch)

Eine Starthilfe für Eltern –

mit und ohne Babybrei

📖 Order now: www.veggieplus.de/buecher

You can download the bonus material here:

https://veggieplus.de/bonus-how-to-start-solids

Good luck!

Made in the USA
Las Vegas, NV
17 January 2025

16606445R00105